Tales
for
the Son
of
My Unborn
Child

Tales
for
the Son
of
My Unborn
Child

Berkeley, 1966-1969

by
Thomas
Farber

E. P. Dutton & Co., Inc. | New York | 1971

Published simultaneously in Canada by
Clarke, Irwin & Company Limited, Toronto and Vancouver

Library of Congress Catalog Card Number: 74-148479
SBN 0-525-21365-1

To Amarylis,
who suggested that I come west,
to those who were there,
and to the
San Francisco Express Times,
a chronicle of those years

There are faces I'll remember

Contents

Tales
for
the Son
of
My Unborn
Child

· 1 ·
Introduction:
The
Education
of Beelzebub,
or,
Memories
of
Tom Perdu

"I saw a harvest moon one time, rolled over it, clothed myself in orange, and called myself a cavalier."

In 1964, pausing between the semesters which structured my seasons, I headed out to San Francisco for the summer. Driving across the country, liberated by the immensity of the land and the sheer passage of miles, I finally reached California. Cheering all the way across the Bay Bridge, I took an apartment with a pool, held a steady job, and spent my free time exploring the area, marveling at all that was new to me. And then, vacation over, I turned east, back to Harvard, back to New England.

Two years later, bound in by the darkness of winter nights, I found myself no longer capable of maneuvering within the protocols with which I was so familiar. Living too much with the feeling that I was remote from my own vitality, I could not take the next step of a progression I had long assumed I would make my own. Unable to give a name to what I was so sure I did not have, past the point of trying to justify even to myself how I could give up such structured opportunity, wondering what to do, I settled for deciding where to go.

There was little rationality in my actions; I simply moved to leave where I was, not even pretending that I had more than a hunger, some hunger. Having been to Europe, seeing no way to build a life there, I turned my gaze west, to that distance, that space, that light. Loading everything I had into a Volkswagen, I set out once again for San Francisco, to where the action was, to where it was all happening. Along the way, shifting moods with each gear change, I had all too much time to think of what I was leaving behind, and I never stopped looking over my shoulder. In time, two steps forward and one step back, I reached Berkeley, and stayed.

Through the next three years the words I heard most often were "changes," "trips," and "far out." I suffered (and enjoyed) many changes, went on some heavy trips, and got pretty far out. By the third year of my stay, having crossed that invisible line which separates one's past from his future, I was capable of saying, and said, that I was the revolution. What I spoke of was the distance I had come and the freedom I had found. People often referred to the revolution as if it took place outside themselves. I located it in myself, and could trace its progress. I felt that I had paid my dues, could leave some things behind, and knew that I had been so much older then, and was, ah, so much younger now. I found, with joy, that I had a voice with which to speak, a place from which to bear witness to my life and the lives of others, a one-point, a touchstone.

If later I was to wonder whether I had learned only that the ocean is salty when one is drowning, if I came to rue what seemed in retrospect my colossal impatience with the progress

14

of my life, I was busy just then enjoying the range of pleasures open to me, savoring my education, trying to articulate the meaning of such constant and overwhelming change.

It is not easy to recapture those times, or their impact on me as I lived them. So much now is past, so much now I take for granted or have left behind. Much resided simply in the calm and gentle openness which was sometimes there to share. Much beauty, if only for a while, inhered in the absence of criticism, control, sophistication, and power. There was an embrace of emotional experience that did in fact widen the range of love, and a willing suspension of disbelief that made anything possible.

There were also fears, times of loneliness, periods of confusion, and days of chaos. Inescapable too was the irony that what promised to liberate often brought only new problems, avant-garde anxieties. I can remember flashing on what proved to be DMT as I crossed the Bay Bridge, terrified that the pavement and girderwork would merge, certain that I would imperceptibly grind to a halt.

I can remember too wearing my Mexican wedding shirt, tooling around Berkeley as leading man in various semipublic movies, feeling larger than life. And even now, when I concentrate, I can find the sapphire in the back of my brain, a steady and clear light. Or I can see a friend being clubbed down at a demonstration, compatriots rushing to ward off the police, all of us scared to death.

Somewhere along the line, through these changes, these trips, in the course of renouncing someone else's renunciations, I began to learn my limits, too slowly perhaps, but to struggle to find the balance. It was such an idea, really, to begin it all again, from the beginning, to personally work through the history of the race. It often occurred to me that I might fall at Masada, or be thrown to the lions, before I could get all the way to the here and now, but I was unwilling to look for guarantees or to take out life insurance. Nonetheless, one couldn't just say the word and be free. To name something did not necessitate instrumental control over it, no matter how startling the revelation.

Watching the falls I shared with so many others, witnessing the enormous gap between our dreams and our prospects, I tempered my hopes, reluctantly, slowly. At the same time, confronted by loss, I began to understand how inextricably we were all bound. In the face of what we wanted to leave behind, in the face of the experiences we shared in that attempt, we became a community. Not, perhaps, the community of the free which we had envisioned, but, nonetheless, a community.

I came to feel that we were in fact the people, *hoi polloi*, in spite of the obvious fact that we each spoke only for ourselves, if often with a single voice. Voting in unison to strike, smiling to each other as we passed by, extending easy favors, we were one. Joined in so many different ways in our separatedness, we shared, for a few moments, a single circle of life, each of us with a position on the rim, spinning in our individual changes as the entire wheel turned. None immune from death, none above or below, we were bound together in the life and times, good and bad, which we created and endured in common.

Confronted with so many shocks, public and private, we could not sustain the pace. The dance of life became a vertigo, we spun into the vortex, and many were lost. Yet we came to share an understanding that this too was our collective experience. As we had accepted our joy as of our own making, so we were forced to accept the pain we drew on ourselves, the pain we had thought we might avoid. We actually wanted to make love, not war; we actually wanted to make love something different from war. Nonetheless, we were to learn, all too fast, if not quickly enough, the constraints that bound us, from within and without. The lessons were often bitter.

Too often asking too much of life, hence too often jeopardizing the comforts of moderation, buffeted about, we struggled to continue. Like Odysseus, the man trying to get home, the

16

man who had wanted experience, we were both many turning and much turned people. Seeking much and much put upon, we were often not beautiful at all, free in no sense of the word.

For my part I eventually lost hold and took a fall, a bad one. I had become a trapeze artist, too enamoured of the thrill, too defiant of the laws of human gravity, and was brought low. Daring the limits, I headed right for the sun, and, as the fable could have told me, burnt myself out. A close friend, bitter in sadness, accused me of giving up, of striking too easy a posture, of seeking out limits which would come soon enough. Perhaps he was right. Perhaps I did give up.

Now I am again a long way from Berkeley, and the distance and space intensify the fiction of trying to speak of those lives and that span of time. In spite of that distance I offer these stories of my peers, my teachers, those who spun on the circle.

It would be all too easy to point to what might have been done, to what should have been done, guided by the clarity of second sight. We all spin, however, on some wheel, if not the one of which I speak. We must all consider our choices, the quality of our life and our dreams, before passing judgment. Not only is life in the living, but one can do no less than to weigh the enormity of what we have all been part of in these years, how we have all responded, since these lives, obviously, had some profound connection to the larger society.

These people left few monuments; their names are writ in water. I present them to you here, and only wish I could tell you the story better. If there are faults, think only that it is the singer, not the song. For in turning back to make certain that they were once there, that I did not dream, I may have lost them forever. Nonetheless, this is my impression. It is all that I can give you.

THOMAS FARBER

Cambridge, Massachusetts, 1970

Randy and Ted

When I first visited Berkeley in 1964 it was pretty, bohemian, and quiet four months before the Free Speech Movement. There were leather shops and coffeehouses, art theatres and bookstores, swimming pools and a general mobility upward to the good life in the hills above campus.

By 1966 eight hundred students had been arrested, and the regents, administration, and faculty had unwillingly acknowledged a new constituency, the students. It was lost on no one there that the passing of consensus implied a struggle of opposing interests, that those interests would succeed only to the degree that they had power, whatever form that took. For those who couldn't handle the social strife there was plenty of weed, and Owsley, the early acid capitalist, labored in his lab to escalate the uninitiated on to more complex forms.

With the end of any unanimity about either ends or means,

with the steady extension of the war in Vietnam as an index of the society's sanity and intentions, many young people were moved (a passive verb) to ever more radical postures and commitments. Postures came before essence, of course, but radical views about the political or psychic order of things were no longer the property of political extremists or social pariahs. These ideas developed from and created a new population in Berkeley, one whose members did not see it as either inevitable or desirable that they could or would move slowly up the hills until they had a view from the top.

These were middle-class whites, products of their parents' best aspirations, who already expected to remain part of the (dis)loyal opposition, at least until the battles were won. When I walked onto campus again in 1966, I was engulfed with fliers speaking to and soliciting interest in a wide range of issues. There was no moderation in these position papers. All the voices were shrill, calling for free speech, abolition of ROTC, legalized abortion, abolition of capital punishment, an end to war, salvation of souls through the Campus Crusade for Christ, and psychedelic diversion at the Fillmore Ballroom.

The area was buzzing with ideas and plans, and in the sunshine, with 25,000 students free to gather at noon, there was time and space to consider all these propositions. On the steps of Sproul Hall, working ponderously, Mario Savio concluded that a strike was again necessary, and Ken Kesey, day-glo bright, exhorted everyone to go further. Finding all this just right, I took an apartment and prepared to continue my higher education.

New to Berkeley, I had only to consider Randy, and to consider his VW bus. He was not at all rooted to the university. Nearby lay Marin County and beyond it, south, Big Sur. Randy saw no reason to define himself as a student simply because he was pursuing, reluctantly, a degree. Too much was going on. With the growth of a hip culture, with the extension and radical modification of the Bohemian culture, with the rise of a large and determined political movement on campus, many people who happened to be on the campus could hardly be described as students.

Randy, for instance, still made his classes occasionally, but it would be more central to speak of the canisters of well-cleaned weed, all kinds and qualities of weed, that lined the top shelf of his otherwise sparsely stocked bookcase, or to think about the jewel boxes in which he carefully stashed acid, speed, and a little opium for holidays. It wasn't that Randy was hooked on drugs, despite the massive amount of dope he could and did put away, despite the amount of tripping he did. It would be closer to the truth to say that he had seen the terror of being alive through his pioneering use of LSD, laughed at the madness, had found a way with weed to lubricate his passage through life, and had decided to do so as steadily as possible.

The slightly stupored manner in which he reacted to the most minor calamities, as if seeing in them the workings of some larger force, this manner initially confused me when I met him. Similarly, the smile with which he greeted anything more severe as though he had been waiting for it to happen, and was once again confirmed in some overview, that smile led me to believe that I had not met his like before, though I could not locate the quality with which I was unfamiliar.

It was the somewhat throttled tone of his voice, the choked tone with which he spoke, as if constantly holding down a toke of weed, that gave me the clue that he was never quite straight. Yet so constant was he in his use of weed, so far had his acid and mescaline trips taken him, that there were no discontinuities in his style to allow me to precise in just what way we deviated from each other. Nor did Randy have any urge to communicate his private vision. He had simply passed on to another reality, perforce shared that reality with others who had taken large quantities of acid, and accepted that he would have to live in an alien world, observing its protocols while at the same time considering it totally insane.

He looked like a California college student, wore corduroy levis, V-necked sweaters, and desert boots, had lines of sharpened pencils on his desk, did his math problems regularly, and had a girl friend. At the same time, however, he somehow communicated that this had nothing to do with essentials except in terms of survival. Without saying it, he left no doubt that none of this garb spoke for him at all. What was obviously fundamental, however, was weed. He smoked more dope than anyone I had ever met or have met since, a constant stream of joints to carry him through each day. He searched for and found different qualities of weed, including an invigorating type that he saved for the morning ride to class, hunching over the wheel of his bus, smoking it down to the last particle, popping the roach into his mouth and swallowing it.

Nor was he selfish with his weed, never failing to pass a joint to the right without looking, always slightly surprised if it came back his way too soon, though he must have understood that no one could keep up with him. More than once I returned to the house to see him sitting there rolling yet another joint, friends lying on the floor, wasted, unable to conceive of how they could lift themselves enough to reach for another toke.

Between endless cups of instant coffee, hot water from the tap, which he used to balance whatever else he ingested, Randy would laugh, mutter about "those dogs, those dogs," and grin at the news of the day. Just what he expected. When times were particularly grim, at the point when every other doper in town was scrounging through sticks and stems to roll one last imitation of a joint, Randy would produce a plump bag of weed, carefully lick and assemble eight or ten wheatstraw cigarette papers, add a massive quantity of perfectly cleaned grass, and roll and smoke a weed cigar, always to the very end, taking the roach clip off his belt at just the right moment, as if to show that there need be no discomfort in getting the full measure of one's pleasures.

He would sit smoking dope, usually silent, it being clear that Randy considered marijuana only a tranquilizer, a buffer he put between himself and enormities he could not confront. Somewhere, some time before I met him, he had flashed on the idea that he was part of a flow that few around him could imagine or acknowledge. The concerns, machinations, and movements of most people were nothing in the face of what preceded and would follow them. And more, in failing to connect with the flow, in insisting on the distinctness and separateness of their lives, they doomed themselves to sham and loneliness.

Even more atrocious, they vehemently believed in their costumes and roles, preening and grooming themselves to preserve (as Randy saw it) a willful ignorance of their nakedness and ultimate vulnerability. They insisted, also, on taking these fictions seriously, on refusing to perceive the few simple characterological archetypes to which they belonged, on not grasping the simple idea that they willy-nilly participated in an unbroken community of the dead, the soon-to-die, and the unborn.

So far was he into his acid visions, so obvious were the truths revealed to him, that he saw no need to proselytize. What he knew implied nothing in terms of action, save a desire to keep at some distance the bullshit that others made the staple of their lives. It was always with great grace and tact that he listened to what I had to say, generally affirmed what I said I believed (except for occasionally giving me a sideways look with his face turned down like the mask of tragedy), and never tried to make explicit the vast gulf that lay between us. It was only gradually, in direct proportion to the amount of dope I ingested, that I got some small idea of where he lived

—inside himself—and came to have a glimmering of his perceptions. God knows he was probably right.

In any case, he had no taste for combat, and read most social encounters as a form of war, though he would never have said so. He chose to be friendly and courteous, to try to stay out of harm's way. Except for those few reactions he could not contain, he seemed both innocent and ingenuous, naive to the point of ignorance. When I first met him I wrote him off as a typical Californian. No sharp edges to him at all. I feared the West Coast would hold no interest.

Several months later, having steeped myself in the wisdom of the fathers, I realized how much I had to learn (though I still assumed that the process was finite), and found it not at all unreasonable to see Randy stumble on the lintel of the doorway and drop a shopping bag full of weed. Nor did it seem out of hand that he should have to replenish his supply two months later. Times were hard and weed was, after all, the staple of his diet.

It would be wrong, of course, to suggest that everyone in Berkeley had addressed himself to the future with so much Mexican comfort as Randy. Somewhere, surely, engineering students still carried slide rules in the scabbards of their belts, fraternity men got plastered in chug-a-lug contests, graduate students trotted behind their professors, and scholars labored an exegesis of Joyce. If Randy saw these people as insane, if he read their lives as very bad trips, there were nonetheless those who could still subsume him, even in Berkeley, like Ted.

Also sharing the apartment, seeking a domestic version of Henry Miller's years in Paris, Ted was an outsider who viewed Randy as crazy. Let his view stand, that Randy was crazy, since it contained at least a germ of the truth. Not groovy, not far out, not a tripper, not psychedelicized, but just plain crazy.

Randy's lingering memory of his father on the roof, baying

at the full moon—that could have unsettled anyone. Or the image of his father's farewell to the world, climbing up a tree to find a perch where he could blow his head off in peace—this too was heavy psychic freight to transport daily. Coupled with his mother's accusation that he would follow his father's unpardonable form of divorce from her, this precedent could not be assuaged or dispelled by any amount of even the finest weed.

Fighting his genes, carrying a knowledge of the insanity of the world, Randy kept high so that he could float down to and remain on the bottom of the kidney pool of his psyche. Slowed, cushioned, ponderous, and fluid, he found it better to stay six feet under than to struggle to the surface. Yet even while submerged he could not close his eyes to the horrors which lurked in the cracks of the tiles. Trips to his beloved Sur notwithstanding, living in the mountains as the Johnny Appleseed of marijuana aside, Randy could not handle the madness.

As Ted watched Randy jeopardize his precious individuality with his use of narcotics (Ted not yet aware that Kerouac's immortal Cassady was leading the psychedelic *kamikaze*), Randy blew it, running madly through Berkeley, throwing his wallet into a creek, handing off his car keys to a surprised senior citizen who became an unwilling halfback in Randy's Statue-of-Liberty play. Randy meanwhile was already long past him, jumping over fences, running across roof tops, heart pounding, trying to get away.

Knowing that no one could understand, terrified, Randy kept trying to make contact, setting up meetings, calling from gas-station phone booths, watching friends arrive, suspecting that something was amiss, and hiding from them. Hiding even from gentle Mary, Mary with the brown eyes, whose gentle mooing and cud-chewing placidity could not wish away her dark skin and black hair, clear signs (to Randy) that she meant destruction to the more gentle people of his light-skinned race.

Randy finally ran to the looney bin, giving it all up, surrendering to what he must have perceived as the ultimate form of bullshit. There, needless to say, he was fed more dope, tied down, and given ever greater doses in direct proportion to his protests that he could go no further, that he could take no more.

Finally, just as he was relaxing to the order of the place, to its antiseptic stability, he was pursued by a nymphomaniac who raped him on the balcony outside the playroom. Freaking again, trying to get away from the lunatics (including the woman psychiatrist who prescribed ever more injections of what he called truth serum), he telephoned to have me come over and visit. Having no choice but to trust me, ruing the risk of each word, he whispered that they were all crazy, that he had to get out of there.

He returned to the apartment, thorazined to the bottom of the pool, taking comfort in the stark lines of his room, the simple colors, the rows of pastel cans. As occupational therapy he meticulously cleaned ounce after ounce of weed, picking out every last seed and stem.

None of this, of course, could wall off the horrors even as he struggled to get hold of it all. He suffered a relapse on seeing a picture of Lyndon Johnson showing his scar, decided to clear out, and came back from Big Sur, eyes glazed, muttering about hippies, those fucking hippies, stoned on acid, fucking anything in sight—trees, roots, cars, the water, each other.

It did not help when his tabla-playing macrobiotic friend Bob told him that the problem was all in the meat he ate, when Bob offered as a testimonial to his brown-rice diet a story about how he had taken just one bite of steak and had fallen to the floor in a seizure, breaking his front teeth. Nor could Randy take seriously Bob's suggestion that he listen to the mantras of Ravi Shankar in order to structure the chaos. Randy knew, intuitively, that Bob was crazy too.

Through it all, the narks, demons of his imagination, kept him looking behind doors, listening for taps on the phone, eying visitors to the house with his head tilted to the side, trying to figure out who they really were. He cut his hair and shaved his mustache, hoping to be anonymous. Frightened, he repented the day he had gone down to the draft board in his BVDs, a huge crucifix set with artificial rubies hanging on his bare chest, telling the authorities that he could not serve because they were so obviously insane. Plotting against plots, he decided to drive his VW bus on back streets only, convinced that people just didn't like VW buses, and would not hesitate to turn him in.

His worst fears were confirmed when a friend was busted, leading Randy to rush to his room, gather his grass, and dump it down the toilet. And just as he regained control, shivering, Mary, faithful Mary, Mary who had rocked him in her arms for so long, who had withstood his paranoid accusations for so many months, Mary announced that she was joining a group of holy copulators headed by, of course, a black man. Randy only nodded. It was exactly what he had expected.

Unable to find peace even in the symmetry of his room, having gone further so far that he knew there was no more, he started the long haul back to those well-oriented lies that keep one alive, on his belly, pulling himself along the path inch by inch, alone, a child lost in nightmares. Getting a little control, he headed down to the Santa Cruz mountains to rejoin the freaks with whom he shared an understanding of the world, knowing too, before he left, that they also were completely insane. He anticipated no help even from his old friend Fez, who was just then living in a milk truck on top of a mountain, determined to get his newborn child off to an organic start with a diet of brown rice. Everywhere Randy looked he saw things coming apart. How could he feel otherwise?

Outside the apartment, of course, lurked real-life narks aplenty, and up on campus, *agents provocateurs* worked to justify the paranoia of their employers. But Randy was in his own hell. It took another year for them to match his fears. Until then he was on his own, waiting for others to see what he saw, to know what he knew. He could not communicate until there was a vocabulary to describe the horror of it all. Only then would he be able to say more than that it was a bummer, though bummer it was, though bummer it was.

Meanwhile Ted, his own torment (being overweight, myopic, maladroit, and lonely) overshadowed, quite convinced that he could never compete with a supermarket-owning father who guillotined meat days and did eighty push-ups nights, knowing that he was of another kind, continued to choose the outsiders as his mentors and protectors. Where he grew up, in the fifties, the only alternative to staying put was to become a beatnik and talk about the misery of being alive. Well schooled by Colin Wilson, Kerouac, Ginsberg, Snyder, Ferlinghetti, and Corso, having early found their works in the porno shops of Toledo, he dreamed of hitching out of town to come to the Mecca of San Francisco's North Beach, not knowing as he prepared himself that it was already too late.

Essentially too scrupulous a person, seeing dishonesty all around him, unable to physically shape the universe in his own image, Ted read books and poetry to set it all straight, to find the answers, to order all the anomalies in his mind, first, before confronting the contamination of the outer world. This process, however, left him ever less capable of dealing with the hurly-burly. Not only was he afraid, but he genuinely desired to be decent and to do right. All this translated into an almost courtly reserve and generosity, an observance of amenities that made him, at best, an anachronism.

Just before leaving Toledo he had fallen in love, put his girl on a pedestal, and watched her clamber down to leave town with an older man. Broken, he turned back to literature, and took it seriously, torturing himself with questions about the meaning of life and the lower functions of human nature. Eyes

27

fixed on each page, he did not realize that he was duped by books which led him into despair the authors had escaped by writing (by not only expressing the idea and getting some distance on it, but by taking the ancillary benefits of the role of author). Seriously concerned, however, seeking the answers, Ted kept on reading.

When he reached San Francisco he found a place less than a block from the City Lights Book Store, stomping ground for the Beat generation, but even closer (a floor above) to Carol Doda's silicon-ripe breasts, the shape of things to come. True to his creed he scorned those commercial bosoms, held in disdain those chemical nipples, even as they filled his dreams, but perceived too that he would in any case never fondle them. Sensing that North Beach had changed, he moved across the Bay to Berkeley, Toledo and the Condor Topless Bar behind him, committed to his *Angst*, genuinely believing that one had to nourish and cultivate his pain in order to transmute and therefore validate it.

In Berkeley he found everyone bound up in politics, dope, and having a good time. The few remaining Bohemians, appalled that just anyone could have long hair, saw no use for neophytes. Ted had, nonetheless, invested too much in his unhappiness to throw it away. Spurred on by the gauntlet of Randy's insanity, Ted decided to show that he could be more miserable than some drug-lobotomized Californian. He would prove that anxiety and sloth were only the gloss on his dedicated search for the traumatic moment. With work he knew that he would one day confront those who thought that he wasted his life, that there would be a day of reckoning on which he would no longer be disguised as mild-mannered Ted, but would stand revealed as *Le Misérable*.

There in his room, the heat off, he knelt on the floor, gave prayer to Jarry and to countless lost Bohemians frozen in their garrets, and rolled back through time, night after night, occasionally taking just a toke of weed (though he knew it was cheating) to push him on, probing, searching, beating his way back through the layers of trivia, affront, and banality.

Eyes agleam at three one cold morning, he roused me to announce the good bad news. In short, he had discovered that at the age of two-and-one-half years, enfolded in baby fat, sitting in the warm tub playing with his rudimentary member, he had been forever interrupted by the slap of his mother's hand.

Having announced this epiphany, for which he had been waiting and working so long, he looked to me for a response. Trying to find the right note, I suggested that it was good that he had figured things out. Now he could close the subject and move on. Appalled that I had missed the point, correcting himself for underestimating my insensitivity, he explained that the curse had been given. His existence had been blighted—he was helpless. It was for his parents now to make restitution for the crime. He would allow them to care for him on money taken from the profits of chopping and plastic-wrapping all that butchered beef.

Randy, just then back from the bin, confronting what he must have seen as a relic of prehistoric times, pulled me aside and whispered that Ted was really on a bummer. Indeed he was, but his problems had to be considered in the light of his telephone conversations with the mysterious dragon lady, a siren who lured him on, cut him down, and told him that he really didn't love her. These charges tormented him, and he of course was quick to protest that he did, neglecting to remember in this give-and-take that he had never met the woman.

One night she had dialed the number, Ted had answered, and, after she had tested him with a few gambits to see whether he would hang up, the affair was on. Her first call was apparently a random choice. Well, not exactly random, since Ted was a lodestone for any bent piece of human mettle. Genuinely generous, seeking companionship in his misery, wanting to help, he was there each time she called, each time she demanded fidelity from an inadvertent celibate whom she had never met.

For his part, Ted played only the most classic roles. Here was his maiden in the tower. All she had to do was let down her hair and she would be rescued. Ted, of course, was the therapist-errant. Deep down, despite his handicaps, he knew he could handle anything. Hour after hour they spoke, marking out the variations of their crazy fugue, her recriminations exacerbating Ted's nascent ulcer. Finally, after ever so long, oblivious to Randy's silent head-shaking, Ted got what he wanted, the chance to see her. It had not come easily, and he appreciated that quality of reserve in her, since he did not care for loose women. As he left to meet her he said something about mystery and the maidens of Arabia, and was gone.

When the moment came she was, well, she was just what he had known she would be, a three-hundred-pound schizophrenic with acne. Ted came home, closed the door to his room, smoked Marlboros and ate pistachio nuts, and was seen only when he emerged occasionally to demand long-distance tribute from the folks in Toledo.

It occurred to him to leave the city, to get off his commitment to suffering, but he saw no way out. It was not lost on him that many young people were going out to the country to live, but he had been raised in a small town, and had no illusions about that kind of country living. And as for something more primitive, well, his feelings were directed by a single visit he made to Big Sur.

Prodded by a friend, he had agreed to leave the cafés for a weekend, and they headed down the Sur looking for a place to camp. As night fell they picked their way across a pasture, dodging cow turds with each step, descended to a beach, laid out their gear in the foggy blackness, and prepared to sleep.

On the way down they had seen a skunk, and Ted was all for going back to the car. His friend prevailed, however, and they stayed by the ocean. The next morning, after a restless night, Ted peered through the fog, saw that the entire beach was alive with sand crabs, and went running, screaming, still in his sleeping bag, to the shelter of a boulder. Of all the luck, it happened that Ted had a thing about shellfish. Shakily, he made his way off the beach and back to Berkeley, sure that his future lay in the city. So much for being on the road.

As his composure returned, Ted began once again to frequent the bookstores and coffeehouses. He greeted each day at noon with a copy of the *Chronicle*, which he read in its entirety, starting with Herb Caen's column. On the press day of each he read the establishment weeklies and the underground press. Later, after checking out the action, he would sit drinking cup after cup of espresso, poetry or Colin Wilson in hand, furtively eying each girl who came in, occasionally even venturing a discreet word. Unfortunately, however, he carried his sense of failure before him like a cross, the girls read the message, and he was generally spurned or made only a confidant after he treated them to a cup of the same.

He was of course seeing a psychiatrist, sent the bills home, and warned me every few months that he was on the verge of a big breakthrough. In the meantime he began to change. He had always groomed himself well, combing his hair for hours and endlessly trimming the beard which ringed his moon face. But now he began to lose weight. He ate only pizza, twice a day, and checked the same penny scale each week to mark his progress. In time he became quite thin, and bought a new set of dungarees to delineate the transformation. But the years of carrying all those folds of fat had induced accommodations no sudden shift could pare away. Svelte as he was, he still walked leaning backward, legs spread, toes out, as if to balance the bulk of his former load.

Finally, as it does to all men, a little success came his way. He found a girl, all eyes for him, duly impressed by his sensitive understanding of the pain we all face, filled with admiration at the way he could so deftly take a book of matches from his vest pocket, roll the cover back with one finger, push a match forward with another, get a light, and offer it to someone who had only just then thought of reaching for a smoke, all this with one hand.

Though not entirely pleased with his girl, still checking out his weight, Ted resigned himself to the idea that he would never have gaunt cheeks, and decided to pursue other forms of self-improvement. When I met him after a lapse of several months, he told me that he was into something new. It was not hypnosis, though he had worked in that field until a young girl he was trying to seduce had failed to come out of the trance. No, he was into something really new—muscular control.

He had already learned to write left-handed and backward, like Da Vinci, and gave me a sample. I agreed that it was very well done, if primitive. Eager to show me more, he explained that he was also working on developing his stomach muscles so that he could roll them, that he was becoming aware of each bone and muscle in his body. When Randy, just then getting a grip on himself, heard this, he said that he had always figured Ted to have good muscles, since it must have required something to hold up all that flab.

The last time I saw Ted he was recovering from a five-month down, having separated from the girl, and was just then starting a new round of cafés and bookstores, back on the search for companionship and power, losing himself in science fiction when this planet got too rough. He was also studying poker, gambling in the card parlors of Emeryville, determined to make it as a card shark. Occasionally, in a good game, he would bring together all his understanding of human behavior, play the strong man for several hours, and show a profit for his labors in life.

We walked down Telegraph Avenue together, heading for the Mediterraneum Café, Ted deploring the trend of politics in

Berkeley, an outsider even there, unable to relate to the pass things had come to since he left home for what was gone before he came, unable to actualize, even in such open times, his real concern for human beings who, like himself, struggled so hard to hold their own. Sharing some fears with me, lighter of step for having displaced some of his anxieties, he was gone.

And Randy? I waved good-bye to him as he moved up the Little Sur River, twenty pounds of brown rice on his back, set as he was on finding something simpler. I am not at all sure that he ever came back.

It was always tempting to think of Randy and Ted as aberrants, and I sometimes did, particularly to the degree that we shared many of the same needs and hungers. Each sensed the enormity of the larger culture, and could not have known that Berkeley would offer only a different matrix of terrors, though it never ceased to hold the promise of another sunny day and sympathetic fellow travelers. And though our paths have separated, I can only suppose that somewhere, right now, Randy is cleaning some weed and rolling a joint, and that Ted, lean behind wire-rimmed glasses, wins steadily at five-card stud and loses it all on low-ball.

· 3 ·
Jerry

I first met Jerry shortly after I came to Berkeley. We were introduced by his girl, a neighbor of mine, and in warming myself in the gentle rays of his open generosity, I came to know him well.

He reached Berkeley at age twenty after years in a very broken home and a brief stint in the army. Without any particular set of political beliefs, long before it was fashionable to take drastic steps to avoid military service, he quietly made it clear to his superiors that he could not function within their limits, did a little time in the stockade, and was discharged. No home to return to, he headed to the beaches of southern California and then up to San Francisco.

In Berkeley, embracing his freedom, he became the well-trusted and well-rewarded protégé of an established Berkeley dope dealer. His position derived from one of the friendships so common at the time, a bond based not on clan tie or long mutual history, but stemming rather from an initial impression of the other's basic being, his karma. Straightforward and eager, wishing ill to no man, Jerry seemed to have very good karma indeed.

In a quiet and unprogrammatic way he accepted the good fortune of having the chance to make some money, and did so. Though purists of the nascent movement thought that dealing was simply a new version of old games, though some dealers had a messianic conception of their role and turned on as many people as possible, and though others sought out the criminal posture to define the distance they stood from where they began, Jerry saw dealing simply as an opportunity.

He was more or less unaware of the penalties for his actions (nor did he know that for a time there were none), he had never seen anyone have a bad trip, he had heard nothing of chromosome damage—in short, it never occurred to him not to deal, particularly since it was a free and open game that most people he knew were playing in one form or another. Nor, given all this, did he identify himself as a dealer. No, he was busy with music, with drawing, with roaming, with people. Dealing was ancillary, his particular connection just very good fortune.

We often sat in his small apartment, a two-room cave decorated in early psychedelic, Fillmore Ballroom posters on the wall, pillows and mattresses on the floor, the rooms lined with rugs and tapestries of oriental design, lush music coming from the stereo, the smell of incense and weed in the air. Sprinkled through the apartment were hash pipes of marble, wood, and ivory, roach clips in metal sheaths, snowmen in glass jars which held make-believe snow, strings of beads, crosses, woven god's-eyes of all sizes, rings, bracelets, candles, and chimes that moved in the breeze. There was organic food in the kitchen, and Jerry provided star charts for all his friends.

We would sit there, rapping, easing through long afternoons, waiting for Jerry's friend Chris to come home from school. Chris, then thirteen, would pull up to the building on his Sting Ray Corvette bicycle, beep the horn, and run up the stairs, eager to relate the story of his latest encounter with the unpsychedelicized teachers who were charged with his education. When he too had relaxed in the gentle bounty of Jerry's place, if Jerry had no transactions to make, then the day would only lead quietly to the next—soft rides on magic carpets.

Without hassles, no particular place to go, there was nothing to worry about. Only occasionally, concerned with the kind of schooling Chris was receiving, unhappy to see Chris go through the same troubles he had experienced, did Jerry advance the notion that something should be done. Those present usually agreed, would change the records, get a little higher, and fall back on the pillows to explore the fields of their minds.

Often, looking for a change, Jerry walked up to the carefully manicured rusticity of the Berkeley hills, picked a likely place to spend a few hours, and watched the city below, the straight people madly beeping and wheeling their cars in frenetic hurry, the fog slowly crossing the Bay and swathing the wounds of city life.

Sitting above it all, Jerry was glad things had gone so well. Though he never spelled it out, he held no contempt for the straight people, a feeling then much in vogue, but neither did he have compassion. There were too many people down there to think about. Discovering the benefits of being himself, of having his being, Jerry sought only to care for those in his circle as best he could. Over and again his friends said it— Jerry had good karma.

In time, with business success, Jerry and his paranoid assistant Fred moved into a cottage and spent weeks furnishing the place. Long hair and pockets full of money, they searched what they thought were the finest stores, and returned to unload imitations of eighteenth-century Spanish furniture, pieces generally marketed to Puerto Ricans aspiring to the middle class. Under these massive chairs and tables, which threatened to suffocate the small rooms of the cottage, they laid the oriental rugs which were guaranteed to be hundreds of years old, a good investment to boot.

For Fred, an aging juvenile delinquent who always entered by one door and exited by another, who never sat with his back to the window, the furniture was a form of war reparations, payment for the outrages he had suffered at the hands of society. Short, myopic, devious in the most amicable way, fundamentally superstitious, a master criminal who always rode the buses (often losing his way and squinting to read the signs), Fred reveled in the pleasure of owning what he thought had been the property of more traditional wealth. A real egalitarian, Fred could see how the mighty had fallen every time he came home.

For Jerry, however, the furniture represented an ordered beauty and calm that he had never had, a stability which, at age twenty, he longed for and was determined to create. He wanted not just the furniture, but the repose he was sure had inhered in the lives of those who once owned it.

When the house was complete, both sat back in the huge chairs with the satin cushions, lifted their bare feet onto the velvet covers of the footstools, and planned for the day when they would have a house that could do justice to what they had purchased. For Jerry it was to be a Tudor mansion, suits of armor in the corners, pikes crossed on the walls, drawbridge over the moat. He spoke of going down to Hearst's castle, San Simeon, to get some ideas.

Settling into the place, Jerry came home one day with a new stack of records, classical music, a choice few of his friends could understand. Undaunted, Jerry put away the rock virtuosi and played Bach, Handel, Haydn, Mozart, and Brahms, slowly learning the intricacies of such time-tested

37

beauty. In this period too Jerry began to consult the I Ching, looking to the past to guide his actions, keeping a firm check on Fred's restless urge to do another deal until he had had time to consult the ancients. Though then in vogue among the hippies, the I Ching was for Jerry no mere fad, but part of his search to compile the elements of a life that would no longer be precarious. Young as he was, for all the openness of the times, Jerry looked for something solid.

Though all was well, friends abounding, money so easy that homilies of economic behavior seemed absurd, one might have seen a shadow of the future—had he been so perverse as to doubt the richness of each fecund day—in Jim, a man of twenty-eight Jerry called his brother. Though brothers by choice only, they were in fact physically quite similar, both slender and tall, both with blue eyes and long blond hair. On inspection, however, one saw none of Jerry's freshness in Jim.

One night, while everyone was sitting before the fireplace watching the blue center of each flame, Jim, who had been increasingly worn and irritable, suddenly jumped to his feet and screamed that he was a dead man, that his teeth were rotting and his brain decayed, that no one cared for him, that slimy beasts were crawling on his skin. Jim was using speed, too much speed.

Jerry spent weeks nursing Jim back to health, sure that with care Jim would do fine, and finally gave him some money and sent him over to his friends in San Francisco. Days became weeks, and still there was no word from Jim. It took a while, but Jerry began to understand that his brother was dying. He took a long look at that possible image of the future, shuddered, and turned away. It was typical of him that he took so long to see what was obvious, so willing was he to trust in life, so full of hope was he, so absolutely clear in his hungers and his pleasures.

All he wanted, really, was to recreate the Christmasses of his childhood, and was, accordingly, forever giving presents, trying to find what each person said he needed to make him happy. His friends, somewhat less sure that the future would not resemble the past, however long the interval of fat times, took whatever he offered with greedy hands, salting away as much as possible before the day of the inevitable deluge. But Jerry saw none of this, busy trying to keep the holiday going, glad to have the money to do so. Without analysis, without guarantees, he assumed that the good fortune he had encountered was there to stay. And why not? There was no reason to believe otherwise.

Several months after it was clear that Jim would not return, Jerry spent the night with a young runaway in a Haight-Ashbury crash pad, and was busted with a small amount of grass. Soon after he was sentenced to six months in the county prison farm. Once there, spirits still high, he meditated and tried to help his fellow prisoners, sad that they were so hardened in their anger, never ceasing to speak gently with them.

One thing only surprised him—the absence of visitors and letters. Making excuses for his friends, explaining to himself why they could not manifest their concern, he watched the blacks and chicanos go out to the visiting room while he sat in the compound. Still, the months passed quickly, he could, as he said, get high off the sunsets, and soon he was back in Berkeley.

Free, he was quick to forget, happy to run with Chris in Golden Gate Park, content to smoke some grass and sit playing his guitar. A week after his release, stoned, he slipped and broke his leg. In the hospital, down once again, he began to wonder about the nature of the world, and even questioned his own karma, but nothing prepared him for the discovery on his return from the hospital that his money, dope stash, and belongings had been stolen.

Limping around on a cane, dope connection lost through the occupational paranoia of his former benefactor, friends unwilling to hassle with his lame pace, he began slowly to try to recreate the days which had so suddenly disappeared. So quick were the changes, so minor the single events that formed the pattern, that he was unable to believe that anything was really lost, that he could not return to what had been before.

In time, leg healed, applying himself to the guitar, living quietly, he opened a small candle shop and began to make a little money. Just as it became profitable, however, he was evicted from his house, and lost his opportunities while searching for another location. Beginning to see a trend to it all, he went to the country, returned for several weeks as if to wipe out a bad dream, and then left again, determined to have no more of Berkeley life.

Absolutely straightforward, generous to a fault, without reserve, unpardonably innocent, his style spoke for the times. And just to the degree that he fitted and helped define that new world, so I met no one whose passage through it was more rapid. Busted, crippled, ripped off, and disabused of any notion that such a life was possible, he headed out of town for the last time in the spring of 1967, just before the summer of love, just before the country discovered the hippies.

· 4 ·
Vernon,
John,
and Rita

"save the children"

It was through Jerry that I first met Vernon and John. Jerry
was busy dealing, and hated to be hassled by interruptions.
When he got down to serious alchemy, when he donned his
rubber gloves and took out the electric blender, when he was
finally ready to buff and cap the latest psychedelic elixir, I
generally took it as part of our friendship to go downstairs and
fend off visitors. Later, when Jerry had made the magic marketable, we could all lick the seer's spoon or pour wine in the
mixing bowl to make libations to a chemical Dionysus.

That particular day I sat on the stairs of the Lincoln Street
place chatting with my maiden landlady, a spinster of seventy
who peopled her cat-filled solitude with her direct ancestors,
the passengers of the Mayflower. So often did she labor me

with her petulance, so many times did I hear of that unbroken blood continuity, that I sometimes found solace in the thought that she was the end of her line.

She had taught school for forty years, and had learned too well to read disagreement as recalcitrance. It was, therefore, always best to agree. Among other sentiments crocheted on the walls of her mind was a repugnance of the wild young people (unshaven, unwashed, unshorn, and undressed) who so proliferated in Berkeley during those years. Even as she gave herself an *A* for both the correctness and the grammar of her point, she looked down the street, said, "that is precisely to what I am referring," and stalked off to her garden to decapitate some foreign flowers of inferior stock.

The aliens she saw coming into view—the sight of whom she might have been spared by a stiffer immigration policy, a more successful eugenics movement, a better Republican administration, or a just God—were Vernon and John. From a long way off they looked as though they had traveled from a long way off, all on sidewalks. If they had possessed an odometer, it would have had to measure in units of city blocks. They came into ever better focus, ambassadors from some uncharted territory, and I fixed my gaze on the taller of the two —Vernon.

At that time I was already overdosed on the regular Berkeley diet of freaks. I had learned not only to accept ever stranger fauna ever more phlegmatically, but had come to find it advisable to indulge in a toke or two of some good weed or hash to help me view this microuniverse with mellow appreciation. It was easy to say "far out," to venture a very controlled wonderment at the richness of creation, to in some mild way acknowledge the outlandishness that had become normal, but one couldn't just glance Vernon over once lightly and proceed as usual.

He was not only far out, he was very far out. An unhorsed Ichabod Crane. A stork without a baby. A barefoot and benign Uriah Heep. Even at a distance Vernon warranted some reaction, at least an effort to precise to just what phylum of the Berkeley bestiary he belonged.

He added to the blessings of nature with his clothes. His pants, forty inches of cloth around a twenty-six inch waist, were gathered and held up by suspenders, and the cuffs broke on thin hairless legs six inches above bare ankles. The nakedness of his head was covered with a soft felt hat shipped direct from some mail-order house in the dust bowls of his mind.

If that were all there was to Vernon, the sight might have been enough to send me to my stash, but there was more. He was surrounded by a pack (a retinue?) of dogs, and the dogs were surrounded by clouds of fleas. The impact of this total swarm, in combination with the fantastic undulations of his body as he moved, made him a mirage in the shimmering heat of an urban desert. He was perhaps the sidewalk avatar of some new plague, possibly an uncameled Oakie sheik.

And despite all the motion, the commotion, it was hard to be sure that he moved. It seemed rather that he mimed movement, that the set around him—houses, trees, and hydrants—that it was the set around him which moved. Berkeley, my part of it at least, was being irresistibly drawn to *him*. As the distance closed, I hoped that we would be spared, that the entourage would pass by like some dangerous meteor in the Superman comics, always deflected (whew!) at the penultimate moment.

But there he was, coming closer, or there I was, drawing closer, and I could just hear him talking to the dogs, speaking quite directly to them in full sentences, as if he took it for granted that they had mastered both human vibes and English syntax. Since the dogs never ceased to circle him, which I assume is what he wanted them to do, I suppose that he could and did conclude that the dogs in fact understood every word he said.

In spite of the monopoly he had going on things visual, Vernon walked just behind the fellow with him, whose position as point man of the entourage made him a human huskie pulling a sledge of dogs. This was John, also barefoot, working off his baby fat in the sun, hair pulled back by a genuine Indian headband to reveal a pudgy face. Notwithstanding his apparent proximity to the open cupboard of a childhood in suburbia, it turned out that John was the leader of the pack.

They had come, he told me in a very quiet voice, to see Jerry. The voice was contagious, and I whispered back that they had come from wherever they had come in vain. They stood there looking at each other as if trying to fix the blame for this particular death march. It must have been that Vernon was minister of leave-taking, since he phrased the good-bye, and told me that they'd be back. I heard what he said, or, I'm sure that I got the message and that he used words, but the point was made in another way. He accompanied whatever words he spoke with a fantastic waving of his arms, made so many movements that I was convinced that he had the arms of Shiva, semaphored his regrets, and they were on their way.

They headed down the street, the last people in town who walked anywhere. Cars streamed by them, hippies in VW buses too, but they padded their way down to the flats, bare feet on cement, making no compromises. Or perhaps the set just made a quarter-turn, and they were once again around the corner, just around some corner, from where I lived.

As I came to know them better, I found that they shared a four-room house in the ghetto with fifteen underage dependents. Despite the chaos and utter lack of fastidiousness or privacy, they had a high sense of responsibility to the new life and to those weaker than themselves. To maintain the house and the lawn sculpture of junked cars, they dealt dope. Or, to go through the motions of trying to provide, they tried to deal dope.

Because they were only just then working out their new ideology, without guidance, because they were doing what they felt had never been done, without any clue to the path, they often lapsed into the forms (ego trips, they were called) of earlier days. Then Vernon would be, just for a moment, a very bright and monstrously ugly Jewish kid from Hoboken, and John the small-town high-school principal's son.

But here they were, three thousand miles from home, supporting a tribe, family left far behind. Cleanliness and routine they had also left far behind, but achievement still demanded its due. Vernon played a few chords on the guitar and John was trying to get his head straight. There was no musicologist to say that Vernon's picking was not yet even primitive, if groovy, and there was no analyst to say that in fact John was trying to play catch-up to his cool and infinitely farther-out brother Peter. Only occasionally did someone suggest that Vernon could not play the guitar or murmur that John "had a thing" about his brother.

It was as if the intense effort required to avoid all subjects which were potentially distasteful precluded any communication save the most elemental, body to body. The language itself, garnered from the ghetto and shaped by LSD, allowed for only the vaguest descriptions of mood and feeling. Facts irrelevant, history unnecessary, the group had simply arrived at the present moment with no particular past save the Original Hassles, and there was no real future save plans to get it together. What energy there was (and it was limited) was devoted to trying to hustle up some dope and some food, in that order. Since scoring was random, since no one ever postponed gratification, it was either feast or famine, but the group had the resources of a childhood and adolescent hibernation to draw on, and it was, after all, a new trip.

Assuming that their similarities (youth and a desire to be free) were the only necessary links, the group sought to purge limits the meaning of which they had never understood, ignoring warnings that had no resonances with life as they knew it. So fatigued by what they considered pointless or malicious

45

limits on their freedom, all those downers, they gave no consideration to what that freedom might cost, and set out in an almost sullen way to find joy, determined to gain the shelter and time to let the world pass them by. They would fashion one of their own.

In the decaying house, euphemistically termed "funky," clanning together as peers, they freed themselves by living in a community where diversity was in costume only. Pulled and tugged by each new fad, quick to pursue the current panacea, they chased every superstition and foible that passed for "organic" wisdom. With the terrible ease of practiced consumers, they went from Dylan to macrobiotics to STP to the Maharishi.

Originally the most autistic among them had been the most successful, needing this new world most and best conforming to it, best able to lead a comic-strip life, to maneuver in such applied daydreams. But slowly the tougher members of the house learned to exploit the lack of definition, and new class systems emerged, almost without comment, as the structure of life became more formal, more stylized.

On the run, needing some kind of base, huddled like cold sheep in a storm, the group lived in a limbo, thinking it was freedom, and gyred downward unable to trace the stages of loss. Always unspoken, desperation increased, noticed best by the ghetto blacks who waited for the visitors to really settle in. None of this was easy to perceive or to consider primary, for the group's confusion was assuaged by the tribal spectacles— the Be-ins, festivals, and carnivals—and by the steady coverage of the media, which created fictions the group felt sure they were experiencing. Surely they were where it was happening, where everyone wanted to be. At the same time, days in the park aside, there they were, adrift. Style did not easily become substance, or, style was for weekend hippies and teeny boppers, none of whom were playing for such high stakes. The life itself was something else.

People came and went, aimlessly, always getting it together, partners changed, children were born, and it became hard to remember that there had been or could be anything else. One of the girls from the house, told that there was a message from her parents in one of the underground papers, showed not so much a callous unconcern as a total inability to conceive of those in a world so incredibly remote.

Slowly it became clear that the new life was the only life, a trap. Those in the house ate organic foods but were undernourished, made love freely but were lonely, lived in constant company but were separate. The freedom from work, from restraint, from accountability, wondrous in its inception, became banal and counterfeit. Without rules there was no way to say no, and, worse, no way to say yes. Acquiescence became the mode. Why fight it? The strongest force thrusting itself forward was accepted, whether it was the hunger of yet another nameless lover or the offer of the newest pill.

The tables were to have been turned, the last were to be the first, but it could not happen by fiat. It took work to generate and warrant play, to make it fun, and excess became obscene unless followed by some kind of renunciation. Trying to create overnight forms that had taken other cultures centuries to develop, the group had only the fragments of a whole life, pieces without continuity, a whole far less than the sum of its parts. Lunging in each new direction, they played, prayed, and paid to excess, losing in each swing any nourishing relation with what went before.

It ceased to liberate, this new life. Worn by too much dope, unable to live the media myth, confronting the transmogrification of dreams into nightmares which became recurrent without promise of change, those in the house could relate to their problems only in the most desperate and melodramatic ways. Overstatement leading to overstatement, some got ill, some were busted, and some went home. Their ignorance and Manichean absolutism allowed nothing less, and in any case, their distress signals, such as they were, went unnoticed. Friendships were ephemeral, and the larger society had no use for those so flippant with what it had struggled to create.

But in the early days, before willful ignorance and neoprimitivism proved inadequate guides to life, before it all decayed, Vernon and John took it on themselves to make the money necessary to sustain the new life. It did not then seem outrageous to hustle dope or to hustle it on foot, though the endeavor was at once illegal and Pyrrhic. The danger and rate of this work were rendered all the more absurd because Vernon and John were middlemen without funds, because their success depended on the steadiness, reliability, and patience of those who had and those who wanted. It would not be unfair to say—in view of the plethora of dealers' raps, paranoia, power trips, burns, rip-offs, and indolence—that steadiness, reliability, and patience were hardly the chief virtues of that milieu. Accordingly, the dog-team expeditions dragged after each shift of plan, struggling to bring the parties together and still leave something in the middle.

Vernon and John brought to this work their honesty. In the face of what 99 percent of the world's population might have considered dire poverty, conditions that might have budged the moral code of most of that 99 percent, they kept their word whenever they gave it. Though not covered by Social Security, they guaranteed everything, everything except interminable delay, hijacking, and their own bad habit of smoking up more than the profit.

Ultimately Vernon emerged as chief of dope operations after a quick and (typically) unverbalized power play. For a brief moment he linked himself to a network that promised him a fortune. Everyone in the house prepared to receive what he had always wanted: a yacht, a Porsche, a farm, guitars, and groovy clothes. Expectations mounted to the point that ever more people were to be beneficiaries of the impending success, though it was clear that Vernon was still in the middle, albeit now in a '53 Chevy, still relying on others to fulfill the functions of supply and demand which would allow him to play, let it be said, the honest broker.

He worked hard to do the impossible, suffering through countless broken appointments with Judd, a deserter from the marines whose stunted life incarnated the worst of the old and new life styles. A liar, a cheat, totally deformed through an accretion of flawed features, ultimately defined by his pinched face and razor teeth, alternately cringing and swaggering, propelled by methedrine and a vision of himself as pretender to the throne of some hellish kingdom, he was a rat, and on him Vernon rested his hopes.

Occasionally Judd took Vernon to meet the luminaries of the dope world for the diplomacy that was to make it all possible, but they found one lost in pipe dreams, another in fear of his life, a third so consumed by his megalomania that he insisted on being addressed as "King," and the rest simply well enough established to have no serious intention of doing business with strangers. Through each failure and renewed hope it was Judd who was Vernon's ticket. They went nowhere.

Though several months of ritual negotiation brought them to the verge of administering a communal land grab which was to be financed through the largesse of a dealer who saw himself as a philanthropist, it was finally clear that the fortune would never come through. The loss was not softened by the criticism of those in the house, those who had been prepared to step forth as shareholders on the magic day of Vernon's windfall. Nor was the blow softened when Bear, the indolent house astrologer, explained to Vernon (whom he called Spider) that he had never had a chance to deal successfully because he was not a Taurus. It was obvious from the horoscope that only an earth-mover (like Bear, for instance) could really get things done. Vernon handed over his connections, such as they were, and sat back to piece it all together.

Several weeks later he was busted. Before, he had treated

such hassles with humor, and even won sometimes. Once, stoned on acid, stopped for violating some unspecified code of demeanor as he crossed the Bay Bridge, he unfurled himself from the car, walked over to the officer, and proceeded to reason with him. Zapping forth a crazy combination of jumbled words and a fantastic waving of his arms, he laid it down that freaks should be left alone, that it was sick to bother people, to be so suspicious, that one should live and let live. And then, satisfied that it was all understood, grooving on getting past the uniform, the gun, and the leather belt, Vernon got back into his car and drove off.

This bust, however, was serious. Driving around Mendecino with John and the dogs, carrying a kilo of weed he didn't need (Vernon got high off the sights alone), they were reported as suspicious characters by a local gas-station attendant who saw himself as a junior G-man. Just back on the road, they saw the red gumball machine behind them, freaked, and surrendered to the inevitable. It didn't even matter when they finally beat the case after weeks of tension and stiff legal fees. Vernon was fed up with being hassled for his way of life.

Meanwhile the house itself no longer seemed tolerable. Splintered glass, flat tires, and wrecked bodies on the front lawn, it spoke for its waiflike inhabitants, those young who seemed to have missed their youth, who had aged too fast, ever more uptight (transforming the soul word from high to low) and apathetic, cutting each other down, backbiting, bitter in never-never land.

The trip became worse as they waited for something, anything, to happen. Those with energy were expected to feed and to cater to the others. The early quiet softness of laziness became a demand for care, as the near dead sucked the blood of the living. It was all one form or another of panhandling. All too willing to do their share of nothing, those in the house could still criticize Vernon for what they could and did term his greed, for his unwillingness to settle down and let it all hang out.

Slowly Vernon concluded that there was nothing more for him there. The energy had been lost. Red, a fine guitarist, went for a year without finding a way to put his hands on an instrument. Bob, who labored for months to build a camper on a truck, finished it, christened it, and went back inside the house to sleep. There was nothing more, unless Vernon was willing to hear Dylan ask if this was really the end, wondering if they were all really stuck inside of Mobile, unless he could comfort himself with Donovan's pretty nostalgia or the lush escapism of the Airplane, unless he could busy himself with endless gossip about who was dealing what and whether it was acid or speed that had blown Dylan's mind.

Years before, never able to fit into the straight world, struggling to get out of it, Vernon had come west, lived alone for a while, and then found a legion of sympathetic others. He had built himself a cubbyhole in the house, painted it orange, and settled in. Yet now, knowing the voids of the world he left behind, having worked for three years to build something new, he found that it was not so easy to just turn people on, to watch them get stoned and therefore groovy. Rejection had made him strong, and he had learned how to do his own thing, to "get behind" being a pariah, but just when he thought that it might be possible to join with others in a community of the outcast he found that this world too only threatened to bring him down.

There had been a time when hyperbole was the stuff of each day, when his very strangeness made him part of what was going on. It had been an incredible idea, really, to think that the outcasts could make it, to give positive resonance to the word "freak." But when the freaks gathered, when the various kinds of psychological and physical hunchbacks and dwarfs, lepers and lames, pinheads and midgets came together, when that part of each person was cultivated and made primary, it became impossible to get out of the side show. Without the mobility of those who came to play, Vernon was tired of the role.

Never entertaining the idea of confronting the monsters face to face, Vernon geared himself for another move, letting geographical distance speak for his private changes, and decided, in mid-winter, to head for Alaska, to test the feasibility of living beyond the eternal afterglow, or at least to move to a place where he could find a coherent life, where there would be no human hassles. It would be different in Alaska, he felt, not because people were basically different there, but because they would be too close to nature, too stoned with life, as he put it, to bother anyone.

Preparing for what he called that winter thing, phasing himself out of the acquaintances he had accumulated, he put the dogs and all he owned into a VW bus with antlers on the roof, loaded his new-found old lady Rita and her child into the back, circled Berkeley for six days and six nights, and finally gathered enough centrifugal force to follow the tangent —in this case, Highway 101 North. Miles later, dogs lost, VW abandoned, on foot by the road, they took a Greyhound the wrong way, but finally arrived in Fairbanks, cold and broke.

They survived the winter in a small cabin in town, and Vernon tried to make it straight. The people who were supposed to be different, however, fired him for having long hair, and the only job he could find in the inflated price economy of the North was for forty dollars a week. Failing an attempt to set up a leather store, living in the ghetto of the few Alaskan hippies, he opened up a less legitimate import business to pay the bills. Nearly busted, he took sanctuary in a local chapel until he could slip out of town.

So poof, Vernon was back in Berkeley, *in media res*, and a fortune was once again within reach, just out of reach. He spent more and more time with his dogs, people long since having proven themselves too alien, too barbaric. Still hungering to make it under the ludicrous garb and felt hat, he was forced to bank on shots that were far too long. Unlike others who counted on weed to assuage the growing penalties of the new trip, Vernon took his tokes summarily. The more way out things got, the further from a way out he got, the greater his hunger became. Without a vehicle to carry his hopes, ever more outlandish, he scurried madly after every hint of opportunity.

For lack of any other place, he returned to the house on the flats, to live in the hurricane shelter of the ghetto with those who still avoided the storms they had come so far to escape. There he made his peace with John, whom he had cut loose months before with the enjoinder that John do his own thing, find his own trip. Out of the context of flush times in which everyone was trying to discover his own special skill or characteristic, the formula (do your own thing) translated into Vernon's impatience with John's amateurism and lack of commitment to the new life.

To get on his own trip John went back east to confront his draft board, told them he was an acid-eating dope freak, and was granted a 4-F. In so doing he made his decision, and began immediately to live with it, starting from the moment he left the induction center and walked down the streets of his home town, stoned, and (whatever it meant) free. He headed for the library, took out a book on Eastern philosophy, and settled down to restructure his life.

Unlike many of his peers, John was all too aware of the enormity of the step he had taken. Full of self-doubt, wondering if he had done the right thing, he looked around him for models of how to be. Student of various yogis, he slowly compiled a pastiche of homilies to carry him on. Returning to Berkeley, unable to consider his freedom a clear victory, unwilling even to assert that his interest in Zen was substantial, he learned slowly to reconcile himself to the idea that certain pasts and futures were closed, certain options gone.

Afraid of the long-term costs of his decision, done with dope, he sat alone, bridges burned. Wondering what it would be like to be a forty-year-old hippy, speculating about who would care for him if he fell, he tested the boundaries of his new life, wandering the coast of northern California, clearing out the disturbing voices, reducing the range of human encounters. In doing what he called a heavy spiritual thing, he worked to see what he had paid so much to get, to discern what was left. Occasionally he spent time with Vernon, the bond between them now more authentic, Vernon fighting against failure, John determinedly slow to draw conclusions, thinking it all through, making such slow responses to questions that no one heard him answer.

Thrown back on each other, Vernon and John also passed slow days with Rita. Still possessed by a desire to make it, saddled with a child she did not want, she had joined Vernon aware that his ego-assertion, though unfashionable just then, promised more than the passivity of the others around her, though she was far too slow to read the full story of his marriage with failure. Her hunger made her blind, her hunger for money, her hunger to be free of the brat, her hunger for a man who was worth her while.

Having failed in Alaska, she lived in the slum, thinner every day, playing at and becoming the witch. If poverty, drugs, and helplessness pushed the hippies on to mysticism, if all the cultivation of the irrational and nonlinear led inevitably to the supernatural, then Rita, with her thwarted and bitter hopes, was a black magician, a witch condemned to the sidelines, working her curses, waiting for others to understand the doom that had already found her. If she was snubbed by those males who would not have her skeletal love, if they reached success in that sunlit world so full of darkness, then she waited all the more expectantly for them to fall past and below her.

She saw no way out. If others could still read the grime as groovy, she saw it only as a snare that trapped her with the poor blacks on the wrong side of San Pablo Avenue. For a while she worked at a hip store in San Francisco, rubbing shoulders with young, hip, and confirmed bachelors. So she came back to Berkeley, drank her coffee in the Café Mediterraneum, and inspected each male who passed through the door for signs of the ability to lead her out of town. No one ever came. In desperation she occasionally "did a thing" with Vernon, or took for the night men who were not really serious, who would not make it, who could afford to dig her child from the safety of their distance. And the child, spoiled, selfish, forever hungry, wandering through the house naked, called out for more dope, mama, more dope.

It closed in on Rita as on us all. The casualty list grew, the busts too many to remember, other less easily identifiable wounds too overwhelming to confront. As the strawberry fields became a mire, Vernon pushed on to Arizona and back, John drifted becalmed through the mists of his future, Rita took her drugs to make love with and then curse the men who came and gave nothing, and Bear, the house astrologist, bulled his way onward to the ever-imminent big deal.

· 5 ·
Politics
in
Berkeley

Hoi Polloi

Berkeley had always had its campus politicos. For years, certainly, fraternity men had taken long lunches in the Bear's Lair (a restaurant in the student union named for the campus totem), for years these gung-ho students had planned how best to steal the Stanford Ax (Stanford was the traditional campus rival), and for years these future leaders of society had been candidates for positions of public responsibility in the well-delimited arena of student politics.

Elsewhere on campus, or sitting in the cafés with the foreign students, the leftists—Marxists, Trotskyites, Trotskists, Leninists, Castroites, Bolsheviks, Mensheviks, and others—spoke of building the revolutionary awareness of the working class, of forming the vanguard without which the proletariat would be unable to realize its historical function. Over capuccino, arguing each nuance, they labored through endless tracts with which they could structure a true vision of times past and times to come.

These campus politicos, whether establishment without question or avowedly radical, found their work well ordered and certain. Rules defined and boundaries guaranteed, there were never any doubts about procedure, and the scope of their politics was confined to those who already agreed. With the Civil Rights Movement, however, large numbers of students became intensely engaged in political affairs, and it does not in retrospect seem surprising that it was Mario Savio, fresh from work in the South, who returned to Berkeley to articulate the lack of freedom on the campus. With the Free Speech Movement, initially an effort to bring civil rights to the campus, the parameters and intensity of student politics changed completely.

The participation of thousands of students in the first campus strike, and the camaraderie of this action, made it clear to more radical campus politicians that there were now masses with which to work. But the games were no longer quite the same. With the increasing use of drugs, not only was there a strong pull to hedonism (which Bob Scheer, radical candidate for Congress in 1966, would castigate with bitterness), but politics, the word itself, spoke to the choice of personal life style as well as social program, and came to imply a critique of those who lived only in renunciation, those whose plans, however radical, seemed not so very different in spirit and structure from what already existed.

No one bound up in Berkeley life escaped politics, as public and private life crossed and fused, as the radical and hip movements met, clashed, and commingled. Jerry Rubin, for instance, was as late as 1966 working on a mayoralty campaign, and, though speaking for the Movement, was obviously running for mayor so that he, personally, could hold office. Such motivation was normal and acceptable. Within a year, however, things had changed, he had done some heavy tripping, and was on the verge of dropping out.

Mirabile dictu, he made a thesis of his antitheses, turned a profit on his past, created a hybrid of the Haight-Ashbury and Berkeley and presented himself as a psychedelic politico, still on his ego trip, of course, but presumably transcending the whole game and himself in the process. Needless to say, it was a delicate link he made, and Mario Savio, with somewhat more grace and less bravado, moved back to private life.

If Jerry Rubin's resolution to the interplay of hip and radical political worlds was possible for him to market in the hinterlands, it was not so highly esteemed back home in Berkeley. Returning in 1968 as a candidate on the Peace and Freedom ticket (with Eldridge Cleaver), he made the mistake of trying to teach his teachers, and was hooted down by his peers, those whom the media considered his constituents. By that time "the people" had come to be those on the street, those who had no such clear investment in their personal careers.

As late as 1968 it was still possible to go to a radical meeting and get clubbed over the head by a point of order, garroted by a point of information, and rabbit-chopped by a resolution to table the discussion. Robert's Rules had taken some radicals a long way, but such protocol, like Rubin's commitment to his own ego, was passé. No one found it easy to proceed, but it was generally assumed that there really was a revolution in progress, that one either got out of the way or prepared to risk everything he had. There were no guarantees.

One has to reach back to remember the flow in which these changes were grounded. The assassination of President Kennedy. The assassination of Malcolm X. The assassination of Martin Luther King. The assassination of Robert Kennedy. The war in Vietnam. Lyndon Johnson. The Black Panthers. The Free Speech Movement. The Berkeley strike of 1966. The Port Chicago vigil (against the shipment of arms). The Resistance. The Delano grape strike. Demonstrations—the Oakland draft board, the Presidio stockade, the Federal Building. Pickets. Huey Newton. Pamphlets. Leaflets. Papers. LSD. Bombs. Eldridge Cleaver. Ronald Reagan.

By 1968 Berkeley had a population of students, former students, and those who had never been students who together formed some kind of loose affiliation, who shared resonances which covered the span of relevant history, certainly no more than the preceding five years. Together they moved through the times, unwilling and/or unable to leave Berkeley, mesmerized by being in the center of it all, slowly articulating the direction in which they found themselves moving, being forced to move, evolving a new style of life, of politics.

As late as 1966 the campus was the center of life for those in the area under thirty, student the primary occupation. At the intersection of Bancroft and Telegraph avenues, the main entrance to the University of California, thousands of students moved past button stands, the Sexual Freedom League table, queues waiting for Fillmore Ballroom posters, Berkeley Barb hawkers, Black Panthers selling Mao's red book, leafleteers promoting and denigrating every conceivable cause and organization, and Hubert Lindsay, an evangelist.

In those days, when the campus was calm between strikes, Hubert occupied center stage. Accompanied by Mr. Sparks, a small man of sixty-five who wore a white sun helmet inscribed "Win with Jesus," and a former sinner named Ray who knew that God watched his every little act, who felt that he was a "dead duck, a blob" without God, Hubert daily mounted a small podium and harangued the lost souls through a portable microphone.

A little man, freckled, missing his front teeth, often wearing blue suede shoes, Hubert would launch into his message, gathering momentum and listeners: "You dirty whoremongers and hell-raisers, I hate your evil, I hate your selfishness, I hate your greedy ways." His audience would stand with half-smiles on their faces, as if they hoped to make it clear that they were only indulging this authentic fool. Heckling, trying to give a better exegesis than Hubert (impossible, since he knew "maybe 70 percent" of the Bible by heart), insulting him, arguing, they tried hard to look as though they were baiting and patronizing Hubert, but they stayed. Fish on the line, he would stamp his feet, flail his arms, hold up a strong first finger, and shout through phrases and cadences which were at once as hackneyed and as original as the sins he condemned.

Though a caricature, Hubert was no fool, and was certain in his faith. Coming from another world, another time, he sensed correctly that the students were in flux, that they would at least feel compelled to argue. Whatever credos they espoused, he knew that few had given a final farewell to their roots. There were sentiments he could play on, lack of nerve he could expose. Still only critics, the students could not muster enough support from their anti-faiths and nervous secularities to refute his challenges. Hubert never failed to say that he knew just where he was going, and though droll, blindly antirational, anachronistic, and simplistic, he argued his formulae to the point that he could play on the anxieties of those who knew what they wanted to leave behind, but who had no clear idea of where they were going.

In time both Hubert and the campus became less central, as the locus of Berkeley life shifted, geographically only four blocks, but spiritually light years away, residing around the Mediterraneum Café, Pepe's Pizza, Moe's Bookstore, and Bill Miller's Store. This area became Mecca for those who lived the new Berkeley life—for panhandlers, drifters, dealers, hustlers, bikers, hoods, finders, losers, weepers, and ghetto blacks in search of something whiter.

A street culture developed, a lumpenproletariat, and with its growth intellectualism was no longer the most radical or vital alternative to the larger society. There was a community in growth, one that had no ties to the university or to any other formal organ of the predominant culture. Those who frequented the Avenue became members of what was unmistakably a counter culture. Having been cast out or having cast themselves out of the larger society, isolated among themselves, they were profoundly out of touch with all save their peers on the street.

The Avenue often served as no more than a place to see friends, drink coffee, and hear the latest news. For some, however—those who were homeless—it was a haven. In and around dealers peddling their wares ("Acid? Grass? Speed?"), politicos planning a rally, and Hell's Angels stomping an initiate or member of a rival gang, one would see the freaks come home, a black man walking up the street holding a transistor radio, wearing only a towel, or a three-hundred-pound girl mincing her way toward campus in a far too small bikini and high heels. Everyone made the scene.

Over and above the spectacle, those on the street eased through endlessly similar days, keeping up with the proliferation of underground news and happenings, leafing through used records at Moe's Bookstore, chasing members of the sex they preferred. A trip off the Avenue would be only to San Francisco, or down to Provo Park on a Sunday afternoon to listen to rock groups. It was a steady life, a continuum which had few landmarks.

Over time, for those to whom it came to be home, their turf, the Avenue assumed a personality, a life of its own as an abstraction, with resonances that unified and incorporated the diversity of its people. It was not strange, then, that on July 4, 1968, the people of the street took possession of the street. After the nights of the month before, nights of barricades, beatings, arrests, tear gas, and curfews, the people held a festival. It was a day of the folk, a day of music, light, song, dance, and mime. It was a carnival, a day of life wedged between more banal and less joyous stretches of time. At its best it was truly a day for the people, a day of catharsis and ecstasy without negation. Though the expression of collective feeling was still nascent, traces of a community, of a broad and encompassing set of values, goals, and, perhaps, methods, could be discerned.

Though lacking the lyricism and resonances of common expression drawn from traditions long held, these street people —hedonists, anarchists, socialists, communists, pioneers, malcontents, and losers—these people made a start. Out of power, sheerly themselves and little more, they were for a moment the children of paradise, those forever in the second balcony, those from whom emerge the more opportunistic, the most powerful, and the more manipulative. Tribute is often rendered to the people, those who die in the charge, who lead unrecorded lives, who make up the flow. But that day, finding for a moment a definition of themselves, the people began to rework the word politics. For that day politics became the sun, the music, the singers, the naked bodies, Meher Baba, the jug bands, the black drummers, the feeling of being able to share all this and see it to be desirable and possible.

"The only bargin is free."

"Brothers and Sisters, follow your own ideas. Don't be manipulated. Don't go on someone else's trip."

"Free stores and selling things don't groove."

"Watch out for those who capitalize on socialism."

"Streets are for people, for us."

"People power."

"Garrison for President."

"You are already God. Can you dig it?"

"Free Huey."

"Don't tread on me."

"People control of our community."

"The last shall be first."

"Only the people are the motive force of history."

"The power of the people is greater than the man's technology."

The day waned all too quickly, and by late afternoon the politicians took over. They could not understand, or, they understood but could not abide the fact that the crowd was after no further struggle. The people without homes, with no stake in anything, had their moment, and did not want to remember that the plague would be with them the next morning. They returned underground, happy for the moment to savor their day, their unity, their victory.

Though brief, the day would linger to be lived again, a suggestion of what the spirit of those who had turned from the larger society could be, what they might feel, might have. Though there was no unanimity, though tactics and strategy (if not ultimate goals) were forever in discussion, there was a coming together, a cohesiveness which would bind those on the Avenue together, which, though it would spare them nothing, would lead them to demand a voice in the politics, in the life, of the city.

Counterrevolutionaries

A response to this new community had been felt in the increasing presence of police through the area in which the young lived, but in the summer of 1968 concerned citizens, taxpayers, home owners, and businessmen began to pressure the city council to put an end to what they saw as the growth of a Berkeley-based Sodom and Gomorrah. Complaining that the Avenue had become a cesspool of filthy hippies who should be in school, at work, or in the army, some citizens, speaking through the conservative *Berkeley Gazette*, proposed tar and feathers for the aliens.

One irate taxpayer, taking the city council to task, wrote:

You are really inviting in more bums, dope peddlers, prostitutes, and other riffraff. God only knows we have far too many of them up there already. . . . I had occasion to walk through them last Saturday afternoon and the whole nauseating sight reminded me of pictures I had seen of a medieval insane asylum. That element on Telegraph Avenue could carry us straight back to the Dark Ages. . . . I will not pay one red cent to perpetuate and encourage a bunch of human scum.

In the period of this expression of outrage, twenty civic groups met in Berkeley's Veterans' Building for Constitutional Observance Night. Elks, Shriners, Daughters of the American Revolution, and assorted past warriors of the land were among the participants. The building itself was like public schools of the forties: it took long poles to open windows; footsteps echoed in the corridors; only the grey-haired janitor knew all the cubbyholes.

The auditorium itself, replete with balcony and stage, was designed for dignified public affairs at the local level. The ceiling was an elaborate twentieth-century baroque creation in light blue and tan. Chandeliers with light bulbs threatened from above. The room was old the day it was finished.

It was here that Berkeley's representatives of the nation's forgotten men and women gathered together. Behind a façade of rectitude and righteousness, faces were wrinkled and retouched, bodies sagged to the center, hair thinned, and blood circulated painfully through varicose veins. Here was firsthand evidence of a generation gap.

The Shriners' Aahmes Temple Pep Band, bedecked in fezzes, played a laborious rendition of "On Wisconsin" as ladies of the VFW, hems well below the knee, ushered helpfully. Notables on the stage tried hard to look accustomed to public speaking. With the entrance of the color guard everyone rose, many with a salute. Women tried discreetly to locate the heart. Some quickly chose a spot near the collarbone. Others, demurely, took a chance.

After the assembly pledged allegiance to one nation, indivisible, under God, after the men took the traditional basso dive during the impossible center section of the national anthem, God was invoked to keep those present full of prosperity and free from tyranny. Then, for some good clean fun, the Berkeley Barbershop Chorus came forth with their routine. Let's bust a chord or two. We'll be hoarse tomorrow, but forget your sorrow. Bring back those good old days.

Finally came the moment for which Mrs. Theodore C. Broyer had been waiting. Her husband began to deliver the address Patrick Henry had given before the Virginia revolutionary convention. It closed, of course, with the famous "Give me liberty or give me death." On the way to that line, however, the speech is an appeal for revolution, something that eluded this particular audience. Patient, they waited for Professor Broyer to reach the immortal words as the band joined in (softly, as from a distance) with the strains of "America the Beautiful." A climax was reached on the word *death*.

Although Broyer was just then getting into being Patrick Henry, it was over—heads bowed for the benediction, and the crowd filed out. Their sons and daughters, impatient with Lawrence Welk and the Constitution, waited impatiently for the chance to get up to Telegraph Avenue.

One of the solid citizens present that night was John Debonis, public accountant, tax consultant, and member of the Berkeley City Council. He was just then object of a recall campaign, and said with a straight face that he was staunchly opposed to the left-wing radicals who composed the rest of the city council. He considered himself an independent. ("I always vote the man; even if you're a commie or a pinko, you can vote for me.") In the man-alone-against-the-forces-of-evil pose that gave him faith in life, Mr. Debonis saw Berkeley as the testing ground for communism in America, and fancied himself, at sixty-four, as the first line of defense against the red brigades.

He called himself a proud flag waver, and said that he

wouldn't mind dying at the side of the Berkeley police. Though one had to temper his words of courage with the fact that he was in no danger of doing any such thing, John Debonis was not simply a character from a right-wing horror movie. He was just a short little man, the only one of his family with curly hair (they called it nigger hair back then), really Johnny, Johnny Debonis, son of immigrants, a man who did business. He was a Shriner, an Elk, a Mason, a man at ease on his turf, quick with first names and a slap on the back.

He was also a minority of one on a city council that had become liberal several years before, and received seventy-five dollars a month to formalize his love of combat. In holding the position he gave Berkeley radicals a bogey man to fight. But in fact, so close was he to an understanding that something in his life was drastically wrong, so possible was it that he would one day ride down with the police to Provo Park and suddenly shake his head, tear off his coat and tie, and let it all hang down, so possible was this that he simply could not be considered the enemy. He was not. For all his limitations, he was one of the people.

Until the second coming, he and other older folk in Berkeley struggled to hold on in the face of the abandon of the young. In Provo Park, in the sun, four old men daily played shuffleboard. The best shot, also an expert on medical affairs, regularly chaired a discussion on piles. During a recent operation, he said, narrating his best story, his legs had been lifted over his head and his backsides probed and exposed to the world. The others nodded in sympathy. They did not turn to follow a young white girl, breasts moving freely, who passed by on the arm of a young black who was fully conscious of how well he had done.

In the times to come, as more conservative citizens continued to complain about unleashed dogs and the squalor of the young, as street people were arrested, as windows were smashed, as heads were cracked, it would be a photo of Berkeley's Mayor Johnson that would best speak for the forces in power. In a candid pose, caught forever, he would gaze sincerely, an older man who (always said that he) understood but who had to do his job. Seated at his desk, right hand on the arm of his chair, expensive pen with cap lying waiting on blank paper, watch on wrist, he would preside over the shootings, the helicopters, the tear gas, the recriminations, and the chaos, he would gaze on and on, sincerely, a man who (always said that he) understood but who had to do his job.

You Say You Want A Revolution?

On the other side of town, not all that far from Johnny Debonis, people marched to the sound of a different drum. A party was in progress, and guests and residents were getting high, floating in and out of sparsely furnished rooms, under no pressure to identify their function or faction. The only decorations were fliers calling for revolution, anarchy, and life through destruction.

The residents of the house, a commune with a varying population, had strong links with a group called the Motherfuckers (of "Up Against the Wall, Motherfucker" fame), who made their West Coast appearance by disrupting a meeting of Berkeley radicals that had, until their arrival, proceeded by the book. That night, strong-armed and loud-voiced, they were more than willing to destroy the meeting, and had angered and frightened the crowd. Whatever they seemed to be (proto-fascists in the eyes of some beholders), their aim was to break down the parliamentary forms in which they felt the Left had become hopelessly entangled.

The Motherfuckers themselves slouched out of the Bethlehem of New York's Lower East Side. With the pride of middle-class males getting the education of street blacks, they saw themselves as a gang, the street as their home. They proclaimed themselves outlaws, writing in a flier that they could "steal, cheat, lie, forge, hide, and kill." In the same vein they said that they were "obscene, lawless, hideous, dangerous, dirty, violent, and young." Not all of this was hyperbole.

They sought to fuse the hip way with political revolution, in their own lives, in the present. They wanted to be free at all levels, and demanded that a revolutionary work to liberate himself from his own traps as well as the snares of society. In this light the specter of death and anarchy they raised was on one level simply a challenge to the games Berkeley radicals played. Revolutions have no holds barred, the Motherfuckers argued, and they looked for the reaction of establishment radicals who learned, suddenly, that now was the time. For the Motherfuckers the revolution was on, totally, and it pervaded even their banter, as they attempted to purge themselves of what they saw as regressions to bullshit bourgeois games.

They lived together in affinity groups which assembled "to project a revolutionary consciousness and to develop forms for particular struggles." In the violent revolution, these groups would "emerge as armed cadres at the centers of conflict, and in postrevolutionary life they would become models for new everyday life."

The literature in the room was apocalyptic—proposing, nay, simply recording the inevitability of a utopia in which everyone could run wild. They had, of course, a list of grievances and statements on the conditions of the times:

the police use their clubs like tampax to stop the menstrual flow of the revolution. the only thing that will stop the flood will be the birth of the revolution, which will be bloody.

They also had a program, if somewhat untraditional:

flower-cong running naked in the streets dangling erections in the face of tourists, fucking each other, provoking bloody flood of police sadism (Inspector Fink, forgetting his public image, sweating over a night stick, grinding it into the vagina of some young hippiess).

It was with this kind of press release that the Motherfuckers made their entrance into Berkeley, as freaks with a scenario of full warfare against the entrapments of a culture ("kick the professor in the gut, slash the Rembrandt, put their Chinese porcelains on the barricade"), as wanderers who challenged the radicals to find where their security resided and to determine its value. What they were willing to pay. Why? Why not?

Living communally, putting out fliers, getting stoned, they came to stay for a while in Berkeley, shocking, threatening, and rapping to the Berkeley Left. At its best, the process was a kind of politicized Zen. At its worst, it was just another form of rip-off, well packaged and done with intensity. Whatever they did, even as they linked themselves to the street people, they were accused by radicals who saw the way to the future somewhat differently of being latecomers to the Left, masochists, ingénues who were proving their credentials by overcompensation. Whatever was said of them, they were certain in their faith: "we must destroy something old and dying, in order to make room for what is new and beautiful."

Until that glorious day when the cameras recorded final victory, until the time Che was played not by Jack Palance but by the Motherfuckers—themselves—they would fight on:

> until our most fantastic demands are met, fantasy will be at war with society. society will attempt the suppression of fantasy, but fantasy will spring up again and again, infecting the youth, waging urban guerilla warfare, sabotaging the smooth functioning of bureaucracies, waylaying the typist on her way to the watercooler, kidnapping the executive between office and home, creeping into bedrooms of respectable families, hiding in the chambers of

high office, gradually tightening its control, waging pitched battles and winning (its victory is inevitable).

If one took them seriously at all, if one did more than find them a not unreasonable counterbalance to Dr. Sluis and his Strangelovean Berkeley Anti-Communism League, if one honored their demands for privacy even as they were the most photogenic radicals in the albums of the Berkeley red squad, if one was sure that they were not in the employ of the CIA, if one decided that such a question was irrelevant, if the narcissistic communion of their Custerism could be overlooked, their unpardonable posturing and cinematic conceit, then one could turn to their vision of a chaos which would mark the coming of the apocalypse:

> when the vast body moves thru battlefield streets
> it walks on many legs
> hungry cells and angry bellys
> guts of anger / blood of anger
> anger on one fantastic throat that cries:
> "now, now this body sees, this body feels,
> this body knows and aches, this body will
> suffer to be chained no more."
> and when the vast body moves thru battlefield streets
> the great buildings tremble. . . .

Given the flow of events in Berkeley, the dissolution of certainty, the feeling that nothing was the same, it was not impossible for one to enter the nightmare. These were, after all, revolutionary times. Whatever the response to the many games of the Motherfuckers, the vision was in no way irrelevant.

Weekend on the Block

It was on Friday night, as the Hell's Angels and most other Americans began their celebration of Labor Day, that the street people of Berkeley held a rally. A flier issued by the Berkeley Commune billed the affair as part of the fight for free streets and free lives, and gave this warning:

know that when you deny us the possibilities of existence, when you bust us for dope or panhandling, when you send back runaways, we will retaliate. you will never again be safe. for we are amerika's children and are everywhere.

In another leaflet local anarchists and communists enjoined street people to use guerilla tactics, to beware of factions who would exploit them, and to burn Shattuck Avenue if they were forced to retreat from Telegraph.

Hours later, after speeches, broken windows, looting, Algerian-rebel trills, bottles, rocks, and tear gas, the scorecard for the evening showed one policeman shot (in the knee), several others injured, one street person with buckshot in the back, and twenty-seven arrested, with a total bail of sixty thousand dollars.

The next day was full of concern. A flier commended the feeling but criticized the disorganization and tactics of the night before. It called for future planning and a cool night. And that evening, police everywhere, was quiet. Street people gathered on the sidewalks of the Avenue to cheer the convoys of police cars, to welcome each one with a parody of the response accorded the GIs who liberated Paris. Small gains aside, the night before, with its directionless destruction, derived from the clumsy gropings of those on the street for a community protected from the larger society, and carried the anger and violence of the recent Chicago Democratic Convention. Desultory, costly, the night had been without program, a nightmare of frustration and rage.

In the wake of the trashing, a curfew emptied the Avenue, paranoia and confusion held sway, and cops stood where dealers once did their work. Meanwhile, factions of the Left slandered each other in daily leaflets. Many radicals, though they did not say so directly, felt guilty about the mob action, and were scared by the terrorist element. The rules had been violated. For their part the terrorists screamed, "Fuck the bourgeois Left." White radicals, they wrote, were three-parts bullshit and one-part boredom.

In all of this it was hard to remember what was being sought. Even as factions of the Left slandered each other, established radicals and the Establishment were locked in combat once again. Like two featherweight boxers tied together, they spent the week trading punches, each side hoping to administer a death blow. Neither could.

Away from the struggles of those who tried to order the madness, street people loitered in the sun, free until eight o'clock in the evening, folk singers and hustlers doing their thing. Panhandlers hurried to finish early, and the junkies were struggling frantically to make a connection.

Down at the Young Socialist Alliance headquarters, the wall papered with posters of the Movement's *luminati*, Pete Camejo posed under a picture of Lenin for the photographer of a major daily. Within several days he and other politicians had planned an agenda for a meeting, but nothing could have structured the chaos of the evening itself. Actually, the night was simply the normal functioning of mass democracy. Speakers were shouted down as everyone who had been around the Berkeley political Left (representing a constituency of their own perseverance) vied for influence.

Provocateurs were seen in every corner. Blacks grabbed the microphone to rap down to the white audience. The moderator fought to control the action. Then someone pressed the wrong button, the stage sank, and the moderator disappeared from sight. Jack Bloom (second most-quoted leader of the Left in the establishment press) was sure that everything was under control even as Hajj, a spokesman for the street people, jumped onto the stage to say that *V* was for *Vanish*.

When the shouting was over Pete Camejo had the floor on a technicality. In his measured words chaos once again became part of a continuum with structure. He transmuted even this mess, through the wondrous workings of his faith, into part of the Movement. At this point three black standard-bearers marched in with banners for Huey and proceeded onto the stage. They remained at attention.

Finally, after the crowd had dwindled from twenty-five hundred to five hundred, the hardy voted it up and down, motivated like hell, and decided to picket city hall and the Lee Brothers Market, breaking the curfew on behalf of the Delano grape strike. What the strikers had to do with Telegraph Avenue was unclear, but guilt about the looting and the wounded cop dictated that the action go for the right reasons, for a good cause.

Out in the lobby City Councilman Dewey, a retired school teacher, fielded attacks as he showed signs of heart strain. Holding his anger in check, he remembered to suffer the little children, and urged those present to join him on that long, slow road to freedom for all men. He was pleased with himself, but was of course quite unreal. A black hit on him for a job, just like that. No way to get around it. Councilman Dewey stepped back. On the steps radical politicos congratulated themselves for outlasting the mob. Everyone salvaged something.

A few nights later, even as the police denied martyrdom to the Left by failing to appear, Lee Brothers took the nonunion grapes off its stands. A picket line—a perpetual linear escalator—carried marchers around and around city hall. It was late dusk when the crowd gathered, and the warm pink light, more appropriate for the Wizard of Oz, passed into night just in time for more serious business.

There were speeches, of course. Jack Bloom dared arrest. Hajj, above the hostile crowd, said that there are never people against pigs, only dogs and sheep. He told the socialists to stop their masochism, to get to work on their own problems. His messages were hard to follow, and he was pulled away from the microphone, but he was right when he said that it was sublimation to invoke the Delano strike, right when he asked why such sanction was necessary, and right when he said that a vision, not a slogan, was what was needed. He alone said that he was lonely and afraid; he spoke to and from the heart. Though Bloom and Camejo called the night a victory for the Movement, Hajj spoke for the people on the street, not for an abstraction. He said, speaking of his constituency, that he represented only himself, a Persian fucker.

Whatever the plans of the radicals, the Avenue was full of police, rumors were in the air, and nothing improved. Still trying to determine just who the pigs were, unable to withstand the desire to elevate the hood in themselves, those on the street suffered the occupation of their turf. Soon, strife ever more bitter, the assertion would be made that, as the Indians believed, no one owned the land. From this idea, like other romantic visions (of worlds long past or never to be) which made so frequent an appearance in that period, only confusion and death would follow.

For everyone in Berkeley, the overwhelming imminence of change and stress left no sure ground. The old and tired shut themselves in, movement radicals found themselves outlefted, and acid pioneers could go no further. Politics, of both inner and outer space, left the body politic worn. Those of both Left and Right, despite the sunshine days, slept with their psyches open to the night, to the separatedness of their lives, to the confusion of events that refused to be shaped. They looked, without hope, for familiar forms to catalog the dangers. Libra had arrived. A new moon. Lunatic times.

· 6 ·
Lenny

Dutchman *is about the difficulty of becoming a man in America. It's very difficult to be sure, if you are black, but I think it is now much harder to become one if you are white. In fact, you will find very few white American males with the slightest knowledge of what manhood involves. They are too busy running the world, or running from it.*

—LEROI JONES, *Social Essays*, "Home"

Do you think you can still be a man and not burn your draft card?

—Question to Lenny at UCLA

With this war, history becomes the intimate affair of each one of us, a private act for which each one of us has to account personally.

—CARL OGLESBY, *Containment and Change*

QUESTION TO DICKY: *In a world with no oppression, what will you have?*
ANSWER: *A beautiful community.*

On October 4, 1967, on the steps of Sproul Hall at the Berkeley campus of the University of California, Lenny, then twenty-four years of age, soaked his Selective Service card in nail-polish remover and ignited it. Holding the burning card before him like a torch, he watched it lose form and dropped the charred remnants. After surveying the crowd of newsmen and students, he explained in muted tones that to destroy his draft card was for him both a moral and a political act, a testimony to his new found and now irrevocably honest commitment against oppression, a manifesto of his integrity.

The students who watched him sever his ties to a society in which they had once expected to function comfortably responded first with deep silence and then with long applause. The males present, trying to somehow differentiate between his problem and theirs, could only stand silent when he reminded them that they carried their badge of complicity and cowardice in their back pockets. Overwhelmed by the performance, by the unimpeachable rectitude of such dangerous iconoclasm, one young man came forth from the crowd to burn his card too. It was a moment of true transcendence. One destroyed a piece of paper and left all compromise behind.

Through the months that followed many young Americans demonstrated their deep opposition to the war in Vietnam and their unwillingness to deal with its agent and procurer, the Selective Service. There had come a point when the war and the presentation of the war had been so hideously botched and so well documented that few students could look forward to participating in it. The war made graduate students of some, exiles of others, and unwilling soldiers or subtle manipulators of many more. Few escaped the issue entirely, though the

76

lucky discovered for the first time the benefits of a bad back or the redeeming value of asthma.

Rejecting the options most others chose or accepted, one small segment of men of draft age formed "The Resistance," a group that had "gone beyond prayers to an unjust king," and refused to serve in the armed forces while pledging to accept full legal penalties (up to five years in prison). Like David Harris, former student-body president of Stanford University, they came to define their opposition to the war as the first step in their own effort to live both peacefully and with personal honesty: "We feel compelled to make all of our actions, the very courses of our lives, conform with the commitment. We have to build a different future by being different people and living a different kind of life."

The question was no longer trying to avoid the draft or to petition for a halt to the war. The first made for complicity, the second had proved ineffective. One could not remain neutral:

> If this war is wrong, then to change the course of this country and free ourselves, we must face up to the truth about ourselves, and then begin to act against the system of oppression. The act must be with our lives. There is simply no other way. . . . We affirm that peace is more than a function of government; it is a way of life that must begin with ourselves, our relationships, our communities. . . . We believe that the most political act in the context of America today is the act whereby we reclaim possession of our lives by the thousands and live our lives with referent not to a corroded political mechanism but to a system of values and an emerging community which we are shaping now.

The goal, then, was freedom from both oppression and suppression, an end to the lies, both social and personal. Though the rhetoric with which they fortified themselves was revolutionary in tone, the act itself, unless performed en masse, was sheerly exemplary. Despite their language (including their name, taken from the maquis of World War II), their plan was predicated on submission to authority. Validating their integrity by pledging themselves to prison terms, they made it clear that incorruptibility was in fact the issue, and worked to leave no doubt in a most imperfect world as to the extent of their commitment to purity.

On October 16, 1967, more than one thousand men turned in their draft cards. For Lenny, who had already burned his card, who had been working for eight months in the Berkeley chapter of the Resistance, the day was anticlimactic. He was worn with his travels around the country, detachedly watching the successful denouement of the once-improbable commitment to which he had bound himself, which he had encouraged others to emulate. Though this public response validated his personal decisions, and in fact pushed him further, he sat a little bored on the morning of October 16, already planning for December 4, the next day of confrontation.

In San Francisco the sixteenth was a warm and bright day, and at noon people began to gather—hippies and students wandering freely, members of the clergy in self-conscious presence, and small, tight clusters of secretaries and federal employees, neatly dressed and curious, looking forward to the prospect of something exciting during lunch. Newsmen and photographers were present, working through the crowd, slowly gathering before the microphone, lending an importance, a wider scope, to the assembly. They gathered on the steps of the Federal Building, a tall modern cracker box, gray, automated, air-conditioned, indifferent—a good place from which to govern. Milling around the plaza before the building, people walked handing out leaflets, selling antiwar buttons, and carrying signs ("Hell, No, We Won't Go!" "Girls Say

Yes to the Men Who Say No." "Resist the Draft, the War, the Bullshit!" "Save Lives, Not Face!").

As Lenny sat by the edge of one of the pools that flanked the plaza friends and sympathizers came up every few moments to confer with him, but he brushed them aside, sitting quietly. Finally he moved to the microphone. Surveying the crowd, taking in the cheers, the songs, and the pride, Lenny asked all the men ("Brothers," he said) who were turning in their draft cards to come forward. When it became apparent that the cheering crowd was too thick for so many men to move easily, one of the young members of the Resistance bobbed through the crowd, a basket over his head, collecting draft cards as people applauded and chanted "Hell, No, We Won't Go!" When the cards were finally assembled, the speeches began, as David Harris urged the gathering to carry on the cause of nonviolent non-cooperation and work to build a new world.

Finally, testimonials and exhortation over, commitments made, the crowd dispersed, leaving only a few federal employees looking at the leaflets and signs on the empty plaza. Lenny spoke with some friends, finished a radio interview, and went home to sleep.

His progress to the day had been a long one, the elements of which he constantly articulated with a fluency born of continual reworking. This ordering of his past into terms which rung almost too true was as notable as the richness of his language. For he could talk, and the strength of his monologues, his "raps," derived not only from his use of language but from the clearly autobiographical cast of his thought. Even when talking about the war he would always locate his arguments in anecdote, in metaphor drawn from his own life. Though personal, his stories related generically to the lives of other young people. Since the Resistance grounded its opposition to the draft in the larger dreams and grievances of young Americans,

Lenny was able to speak to the lives of his peers through tales of his own struggles to find himself.

The care with which he organized his past and the precision with which he derived his politics from his life history belied a background from which he selected incidents to help him define the present, to act as his own historian and read in his life an undeniable continuity. If this process betrayed a fragility in his commitment, it did not function negatively in his interaction with his peers, particularly in a student community in which the values of the adolescent were cherished, where iconoclasm and commitment to dreams were at least as highly esteemed as more substantive achievement.

Lenny spent day after day urging others to join them, criticizing what he saw as their lack of courage or honesty, drawing them to his world view through conversation. He held court, endlessly, talking quietly when he felt he was uttering a truth, a faint smile playing on his lips as he passed the truth on, the smile now ironic, now patronizing, now self-conscious. Often he did not try to convert others at all, content rather to record the immaculateness of his own position, expressing the abandon to which he had become entitled. Given the weight of draft cards in their wallets, obsequious letters asking for deferments, banal classes, papers, exams, given also a general admiration for pyrotechnics, the students who listened to Lenny generally envied the freedom he had gained. No one was able to estimate what the price of that freedom would be.

As Lenny talked he spoke with his hands, sweeping them smoothly, molding his ideas, making his points with right forefinger extended, the whole process fluid, soft, and graceful, if well rehearsed. The theatrical gestures, slightly fey, matched the personnae he adopted, from the enforced coarseness of the nightclub comic to the self-consciously delicate sincerity of the revivalist, all in the cadences of a New York Jew. Often he was simply crude, yet he turned crudity to advantage, as if daring his listeners to be put off, ready to let them remember that he was of course purer than they had the courage to be. He had manifested his integrity; he could expect his lapses to be excused.

Occasionally he reached points in his raps when his word pictures, his incredibly telling anecdotes, left his listeners hanging on his images, caught by his capacity to strike resonances in their own lives as he talked about himself, moved by his ability to elevate the small wins and losses of growing up into the stuff of saga. There was Lenny in the locker room after the football game, uniform still clean, trying to find some mud, or Lenny planning to set up a wedge of chairs in the exam room for himself and his friends, the better to pass on answers, only to find a nun sitting in the fulcrum of his formation.

The stories were full of self-deprecation, he took his pratfalls, but the total effect was to aggrandize the life, to transform, in the telling, the confusion into order, the debacles into manageable memories. And when he had his audience, when they waited on his every word, he could turn the irony from himself to others, and bring low even the mighty. Woe to the public figure who caught his eye, for he could see even the illustrious with their pants down, and immortalize their bare bottoms.

So Lenny rapped, seldom losing control, bringing the world into his domain by his ability to comment on it. In a community of the young, where words were often the only measure of one's freedom from the past and promise for the future, Lenny was a brilliant performer, no less than a whole man.

He sat on campus, talking on the same themes, using the same anecdotes, seldom incorporating anything new. It was as if at twenty-four he had come to terms with his past and was now devoting himself to the task of telling what he had learned thus far, defining himself as a person who had learned how to define himself. Given the movement of life in Berkeley, the constant arrival of yet another cult, fad, or posture, it took a great deal of subtlety and effort to brave the criticism of others and hold sway.

But hold sway he did, in constant trial by conversation, standing about six feet tall, of medium build, sometimes tending to paunch, with fairly sharp features, a sharp nose, thin lips, and blue eyes. His complexion, faithful recorder of psychic stress, retained scars of earlier battles with acne, bearing witness to the difficulties of getting over the troubles of being young. Though his face was not strong, cheeks and throat a little fleshy, he was good looking, like a matinee idol in a studio photograph, glossy and retouched. With his long, thick black hair he resembled a composite of Cliff Robertson and Tyrone Power.

In that period he often wore relics from college styles of the past—saddle shoes, white socks, powder blue jeans, and a tennis sweater, fortifying himself against the cold with a navy jacket, collar upturned. As time passed he slipped into hippie garb, striped pants and handmade shirts, then almost a deliberate breach of protocol for a student activist.

Above all, however, he seemed to be aging, a little old in comparison with those he attracted most. Sitting and talking on campus before an inevitable group of listeners, slightly patronizing to males he considered inferior and to women, for whom he was always on the watch, he passed his days expounding his definition of himself. To the degree that no one had or would communicate any such clarity about themselves, he was considered an authority. Speaking paternalistically of the younger members of the Resistance, always ready to be distracted by some new presence, reaching to receive an embrace from those to whom he felt close, at once distant and completely engaged, he dominated the scene.

The stance that he worked so hard to make viable had been preceded by years of searching. Born in New York City, son of a father who worked hard and died too soon, he started at seventeen a six-year period in which he attended pharmacy school, acting school, film school, college, and a Peace Corps summer training session. He completed none of these programs. Though he initially did well at pharmacy school, he was dissatisfied, turned to fraternity games, and was thrown out of school after setting a campus record for mooning, or bare-assing, a fraternity contest then popular in which the goal was to expose the buttocks in public as inventively as possible. As Lenny recounted the incident, he took the title by executing the nearly impossible half-moon with a shooting star.

At film and drama school, playing the role of the Hollywood hippie, he was still dissatisfied, unable to work through the programs. He left, tried the Peace Corps, quit, and arrived in Berkeley as a twenty-three-year-old freshman. He had come a long way, and in ideology had nothing good to say about what he left behind. He argued that he retained from his past only a feeling for lives filled with compromise, people afraid to live. He did not want to die like his father, overworked, overextended, and unfulfilled. In anecdote, however, he expressed a less critical view, making clear that he enjoyed aspects of middle-class Jewish life, that he didn't mind fraternity life, and sometimes sounded as though he would have liked nothing better than to take the Peace Corps on its own terms. Nonetheless, he had sought out more dramatic and compelling work for himself, and had landed in Berkeley.

Somewhere during those six years when he was searching for a suitable role in which to invest, he listened to the records of Lenny Bruce and armed himself for his battles with worlds he first coveted and then cast away. From Bruce he learned to define hypocrisy, and shared with him the iconoclastic innocence of the revelation. Bruce's influence was to stay with him as he constantly played Bruce's bits, slowly becoming original with Bruce's model. Finally, in 1966, at the moment that he entered Berkeley student politics, he introduced himself as Lenny (not as Stuart, his given name, nor as Tony, his acting name). Although he entertained an audience that night, keeping them in good spirits, he had more than humor on his mind. He had found with Bruce that to parody, to know the lies, was not enough.

What Lenny took from Bruce's life was that even at the peak of his success as a comedian, Lenny Bruce, nee Schneider, had still not completely adopted his new identity. He was still groping for acceptance, even as he innovated. It was not until Bruce became entangled in the legal problems of his obscenity cases that he concerned himself with the right to express himself publicly in idioms used privately by the general public. In the course of his trials Bruce ceased to function as a comedian and devoted himself to a quite humorless war against repressive statutes.

In Berkeley the night that Lenny took a new name (hence, as he saw it, a new identity), a strike was about to begin, and Lenny found for the first time a cause that could engage him:

> I had been sort of drifting on the periphery of the strike for a while, and when the issue of the steps * came up, I was incensed; that was too much, that was a personal affront. That wasn't going to happen. I was going to do something . . . but that wasn't going to happen, that was it. I felt that someone ought to say, well, if they pull that shit we'll just shut down the motherfucker. That's all. I had no fears at all of being kicked out. In fact, it wasn't a bad idea.

That night was the occasion of my first encounter with Lenny. The meeting had been called to give unaligned stu-

* Preceding the strike, there was a lengthy controversy between the administration and student activists over whether or not student groups could continue to hold their rallies at noon on the steps of Sproul Hall, directly in the center of campus. The administration's eagerness to move the rallies to a less central location met the bitter opposition of student radicals who felt that such a move would vitiate their ability to speak easily to large audiences.

dents on campus an opportunity to discuss the issues that threatened to bring on yet more disruption. Though more radical students intended to guide the meeting, Lenny jumped on stage to help keep the meeting democratic. Making the audience laugh, mocking the manipulations of those who tried to get him off the platform, handling comments and suggestions with imparitality and brilliant comebacks, getting into blue humor and nightclub patter to control those who tried to roll over the majority with procedural tactics, he was a verbal Robin Hood.

One critic, impatient with mass democracy, started to censure him, but Lenny broke his argument to say, "Excuse me, sir, your fly is open." An old line, crude too, but the man looked down, realized that he'd been had, and retired. One-liners notwithstanding, Lenny was serious, trying to encourage the gathering to do the tedious work of getting together, insisting on fair play. He was in great form, and I had never seen anyone like him.

When the strike was finally set in motion, he found himself in the midst of what seemed a new world in the making. Daily mass meetings culminated in a rally chaired by Mario Savio in which five thousand students responded by acclamation to his motion for a strike. For a brief time the enthusiasm of the Free Speech Movement was recaptured, and the students once again had hopes of restructuring the university. Beyond the immediate issues of the arrests, the war, and free speech stood the dream of recreating the educational system. To this end there were countless and endless meetings, picket lines, fliers, buttons, megaphones, and songs.

In this period Lenny found both a community of the discontent and a specific enemy. From this experience he saw firsthand what political activism looked like and felt like, and he was pleased. Taking personally the strongest words spoken in the strike, he resolved to put his life on the line and join the embattled. The strike itself, however, ended in frustration. Student leaders were sentenced, the chancellor ignored student demands, and students stopped picketing to study for their exams. But Lenny transformed his personal frustrations into ideology; he had found a cause and a context. As he said, he had nothing to lose, and something real was happening.

Though the language of the strike was inimical to the larger society, the strike itself fostered a rapport, however brief, that stood in sharp contrast to the normal fragmentation of lives in Berkeley. What attracted Lenny so deeply was deviant in the larger scope of American society, yet in Berkeley it was a world of great enthusiasm and *élan*. Not only did sheer energy and commitment seem enough to make change, but the side benefits of being an activist were substantial. It was a way to live.

Five months later Lenny became one of the founding members of the Berkeley chapter of the Resistance. Tired of his fear of the draft, committed to political activism, drawing on conversations with an Indian who had told him that the war could be stopped by a nonviolent movement of draft resisters, Lenny was primed for the task. Though the strike had failed, Berkeley still treated activists with respect. Looking for something in which to invest, searching for opportunities to use his energies in a community which offered few roles other than student, outraged by the flow of political events, unwilling to be pushed by the Selective Service, Lenny launched his crusade.

Initially he teamed up with a Berkeley radical who had reached his politics through a sober intellectual examination of political affairs, who had already paid his dues in the Movement. They were, needless to say, an unlikely pair. Lenny's flamboyance stood in sharp contrast to his cofounder's earnest socialism, but together they began to write fliers, working out of Lenny's dingy rented room, a poster of Lenny Bruce on one of the black walls, and soon attracted kindred spirits.

Within weeks, however, Lenny's partner quit, writing in a

socialist publication that the Resistance was just another kind of moral commitment "designed to stir one more wave of middle-class sentiment against the war and American militarism," a form of moral witness not calculated to foment real social change. Though hurt, Lenny was no ideologist, and was indifferent to considerations of strategy or tactics. Suddenly endowed with the impeccable credential of clear commitment to action, he had found a pose—straight, simple, self-sacrificing—that satisfied him, a definition which, like none other he had tried, measured up to the romantic vision that was his reading of life.

In the early months of this work he became, as past actor, the revolutionary's revolutionary. Dressed in high black boots, listening to records of the Red Army Chorus, Lenny spoke of "the people." Even as he had been too quick to become Tony, the consummate unemployed film-maker, or Lenny, a new Lenny Bruce, so at first he overplayed his role. He had yet to validate what he still only half-believed, what was not yet integral. Laboring through the chasms between past life, present convictions, and future action, always aware of good theater, he stood as a Hollywood version of what he hoped to become, hyperbolic, spouting diatribes that sounded like parodies of leftist rhetoric.

In time he became more authentic, and with less effort was able to read his noncooperation with the draft as a metaphor for his life. Such history was revisionist, of course, but confirmation for the view was ever more available, through confrontations with draft boards, induction centers, local police, with FBI surveillance, (probably) tapped phones, and the arrests of friends.

As the months passed, Lenny became more secure in the role of *kamikaze*, even happy. Whatever the ambiguities in such a resolution, he was entitled to bravado, and walked around like the Englishman who will at any moment don a silk scarf and take up a plane against overwhelming odds.

Gathering surety and status in a subculture which measured individuals by the degree of their commitment to political opposition, he profited also from his feeling that he was free of the compromises that shaped the lives of others.

Inevitably, too, there was paranoia, a word that was central to Berkeley life in this period. Whatever debilitating effect such fear had, it at least endowed antiestablishment efforts with importance: someone cared enough to hate. At the same time, this shared fear brought the members of the Resistance closer together. There were risks, and all faced these risks in common. That was a fraternity that made sense.

For Lenny the role of revolutionary necessitated constant awareness:

> If you want to be a revolutionary you have to be awake, you can't have one minute's peace, you're alive every single moment. . . . When you hear a sound, the sound of the wind, the footsteps right at the door—not a wasted motion. It is intense, and there are distortions that take place under that intensity. When you see a cop you have to size him up. I mean he's the enemy, and every time the Gestapo walks in, you go through changes. It's a very scary feeling to think that every phone is tapped, so it's not tapped, it's just the idea that you have to be conscious of that, you feel that there's a microphone, you know there's been too many investigations. Every place I go someone has talked to the FBI.

Though never given to understatement, Lenny lived these words. The punishment, he feared, would fit the crime. And he knew that he was becoming a criminal, or an outlaw—depending on how you saw it.

For all the paranoia of these days, for all the hard work, there were many good times. The constant flow of people crashing in the room, if exhausting, gave Lenny countless opportunities to rap to and convert others. Beyond the hassles, there were nights when he would take out his guitar and play Dylan songs, sitting before his friends, singing them the words of the master. He had come far enough to warrant nostalgia, and could sing with honest sadness the bittersweet lines of "Love Minus Zero/No Limits." At these moments, tasting loss and camaraderie, those in the room were warriors all, outcasts who felt their own capacity for heroism. It did not then seem out of place to adopt a special handshake, a three-phased clasp that confirmed the solidarity of the initiated.

Along the way, writing off the most limiting aspects of his Jewish heritage, free with criticism of the Israeli state even as he located his raps in the style and inflection of Lenny Bruce, Lenny passed through what was to become *de rigeur* for white radicals—the use and knowledge of black language, movement, and song.

His guide to the black world was his friend Dicky, a black with good radical credentials, since he had been an organizer in the South with a purported battle record of eighty-seven arrests. The day was not far off when Dicky would have to defend his obvious pleasure in spending so much time with white folk, but for the moment he was Lenny's good friend and teacher.

Even as Lenny learned soul dances, how to give the clenched fist, and the proper technique to carry off the slapping of palms, a ritual not easily learned after years of handshaking, he understood that he was in fact not black, that he could not (and had no desire to) absorb the violence of the ghetto. What he did feel was that in relation to the larger society he was in the status of a black man, albeit a middle-class black man, since he was polite.

Dicky also gave him—beyond some feeling for those who lived with oppression all their lives, beyond the status of the soul gestures, past the aura of blackness that helped Lenny gain distance from the larger society—good counsel on the problem of questioning at the psychological level, the old middle-class hang-up. Dicky was primarily interested in getting things done, a refreshing outlook for Lenny to learn, despite the obvious fact that Dicky had a fairly intense obsession about white girls. In any case, Dicky knew people, hustled, understood fear, and felt compassion. Around him it wasn't going to be so easy to speak of St. Juste or Robespierre.

In Dicky, Lenny had found another teacher, and was eager to learn. Still searching for authenticity, Lenny looked for guidance from those who had a clear sense of purpose and identity, like Mario Savio, like David Harris, like Dicky. In the months that followed, Dicky's imprint was felt in the group, as "the people" became "the brothers." It was a linguistic shift, to be sure, but the word expressed a truth, for in this period Lenny worked to create a community of the outcast, a world in which those against the war could be members of some cohesive opposition. He struggled to define a context in which love and community could be expressed, where the roles of manhood would be vital. In the company of those who refused to serve, he found the common sacrifice and dedication that he felt were the necessary components of a new way of life. All those who passed through what he called the land of fear were to be as close as brothers, and warranted from each other concern and tolerance, care they felt they had never before received, or, perhaps, merited.

The specifics of this world-to-be were never articulated with any precision, but were presumed to be rooted in some kind of anarchic socialism. The ideology of the group, such as it was, centered in its slogan, "Do it!," for "it"—the act of refusing to serve—stood above all else. The act alone entitled (indeed, required) the individual to reshape his life. The directness of this simplistic approach baffled and angered other antiwar groups, whose representatives considered the Resistance inexpedient or suicidal. Uninterested in the complexities of things political, however, the Resistance asserted the need for unambiguous action. Sealing their pact in their own blood, their concern was for those who dared to join them.

Though in practice honored as much in the breach as in the observance, this concern became central to the ideology of the Resistance. For Lenny this involvement with each life made him uneasy about his role as proselytizer. Nonetheless, though he felt for those who joined the group, though he often said he would urge them to leave the country rather than face prison, he continued to recruit. At the same time, however compelling his rhetoric, he was overwhelmingly bound up in his own changes, most happy with those who either deferred to him or who could sustain his pace. He continued to speak endlessly about community, about the creation of a world that would assuage loneliness and pain, yet steadily he took more than he gave. Closest with the strongest members of the group, he was unable to offer more than a moment of consolation or laughter to the others, almost unaware of the distance between his rhetoric and his capacity to personally render the words real.

In time, even the paternalistic distance he kept between himself and the younger members of the group did not suffice. Tired with an endless round of partners for the night, he had found a girl with whom he wanted to live alone, away from the other members of the group. He turned too to other interests, experimenting with films, leaving the group (now in a commune) on its own. He still could and did say "the power of the people is greater than the man's technology," but he was tired of the daily work of the group, unable to make himself invest in each new member, and more, unable to sustain the immaculateness of the moment in which he had burned his card. Waiting for something to happen, living in a restless limbo of expectation, watching days pass, now in Chicago, now in Washington, now in New York, he failed to be able to fix himself in the apocalyptic moment, and could no longer taste the feeling of being matador in the political arena.

Away from the razor's edge he felt inadequate, and said that the younger members of the group had gone past him, even if they were slow to realize the fact: "Now I see them, and they look at me with scorn and disdain, now I know that they feel about me as I felt about Savio. I'm not perfect, and they have this view of perfection. Now the mystery is gone." Though it was *his* view of perfection and *he* who felt the loss of mystery, a time for parting had indeed arrived. Still unwilling to live with the group, he came no closer to being able to supply the care that younger members of the group felt he had promised them. Hurt, they grew impatient.

Trying to find his ground, Lenny thought for a while that he might follow the path of David Harris and continue to spend his time traveling and speaking about non-cooperation, but instead he decided to stay in Berkeley, to work on local radical politics in the community. Endowing himself with the role of local rabble rouser, the perpetual gadfly, he planned to help the street people and students without taking on power or responsibility.

Increasingly remote from the resistance community that he had helped to create, he was still an exhibitionist, unable to market himself as a daredevil to those who shared the same risks, not yet ready for the drudge work of building slow relationships, of realizing no miraculous gains. At the same time, he was genuinely disappointed that radicals weren't much different from anyone else. Having entered yet another new world, having risen so fast in it, having met Tom Hayden, Dr. Spock, Joan Baez, and other radical luminaries, he reached the top only to find petty rivalries, confusion, and backbiting. Still waiting for the moment of truth, without its clarity, having joined with the faithful, having established himself, he found once again that nothing matched his image of what it would be.

In this period we met often, exchanging stories and news, Lenny irritable and at odds with himself. Only occasionally did he shake off his gloom to joke, to tell me about how he tried to separate two fighting dogs with his karate, getting for his pains only two surprised dogs and an injured foot. For just a moment the humor of the situation was real, one of the anomalies of life he could render so well, but then he returned to his own thoughts, preoccupied, remote, distant. Lenny had always talked about himself, but in the past his autobiographical raps were invitations to others to empathize, to join with him in common feeling. Now, though he was still his own chief concern, there was no way to share with him, so deep was he in self-pity and very private turmoil. He had lost the capacity to make metaphor of himself, his most precious gift.

Primary in his thoughts was prison. Knowing almost nothing at all about what he would face, taking his lead from Edward G. Robinson and James Cagney, he was ready to laugh when they put the handcuffs on him, ready to laugh all the way until he was lost from the sight of the faithful. It was a grade-C movie, of course, but his own. Despite the bravado he envisioned, however, he was increasingly pessimistic about the role of his martyrdom. Thinking about the future, he saw himself getting out of prison after five years only to be called an Uncle Tom by those who would ask why he had been nonviolent. As the revolution grew ("people will be in mass revolt, whole cities will be wasted. . . . the country will shake and shake and shake and fall apart because it's rotten"), he would be unprepared to see it since he had "come in at the wrong stage, when things were too slow, when people were not really fighting."

Given his feeling that he would soon be a relic of a conservative past, despite his statement that even a leftist revolution would purge him, suddenly everything changed. The conspiracy trial of Dr. Spock discouraged the government from further prosecutions of that sort, and, taking his induction physical, Lenny was sent home before he reached the line he said he would not cross. After all the months of work, after all the speeches and conversations, after all the posturing, anxiety, and waiting, he didn't have to "do it" at all. He was, suddenly, a free man.

Free? Free once again to work to some definition of himself, to confront his life rather than the promise of his death, free to live with those whose lives were perforce filled with compromise. He spent no more time in politics, finding himself impure, and in fact he no longer had a dramatic posture within which to structure his efforts. No longer beyond self-criticism, he had once again to accept his fallibility, his most undramatic fallibility. Without the photo finish of the ride to prison, with the script changed, he had to choose another movie.

No longer a romantic hero in the company of the liberated, far from the ultimate risk of living death with which he had been obsessed, unable to see how he could make the leap to the role of revolutionary willing to die without the prison experience to harden him, he could still assert that the entire system was out of joint, but was no longer committed to total change insofar as he had no clear vehicle for immolating himself in the inferno that was to precede paradise. Though no one held it against him, though all repression was now mild enough to allow more moderate resolutions, Lenny had no idea of which way to go.

Free of his role, he became rehumanized, beginning again to show concern for others, telling stories once more, making others and himself laugh. Traveling, waiting for a new definition, he dressed ever more carefully, natty in hip garb, an updated version of Tony, Hollywood Tony.

In the months that followed he was steadily less frenetic, writing occasionally for an underground paper, spending more time with women, working through the changes that passed through town. Always compelling, always driven to others and able to involve them in his interminable personal struggles, Lenny had to learn to live more quietly. Everyone in Berkeley was trying new paths, and he had no special claim vis à vis the efforts of others to find their way. Even with women, to whom he had always been so attractive, so many of whom he had passed through with such ease, he had to learn accommodation. The role of males was being reevaluated in Berkeley; he was accused of being a chauvinist.

Laboring through prosaic days, writing about the changes, he searched in his prose for the ever-imminent civil war. Through a series of columns for his paper he articulated his vision of the day Berkeley would rise, presenting a radical Western entitled "Berkeley Guns," in which the Left finally got it on. Given the bombings, the arson, the shooting of police, and the entrenchment of many Berkeley residents in a well-defined subculture completely hostile to the larger society, it was not an entirely fanciful scenario. Life following art, as it always did for him, he readied himself for the day.

Through all of this he continued to lead the Berkeley life, hustling on the Avenue, seeing friends, making the rounds, stopping just short of the revolution, staying just inside the enforceable law. No longer immaculate, no longer on the verge of sacrificing his life, he bid a final good-bye to the accouterments of a man about to go to prison. Conceding some of his rhetoric and absolutism, he lived each day and each week with the rhythms of other folk, sharing with other Berkeley residents a feeling of nesting in the eye of the hurricane, but doing it, day by day. Some storms over, he learned to live with himself until the apocalypse materialized: "I wanted to be a rebel, a revolutionary, and [*pause*] I'm still me, and I don't know if anybody could tell the difference." There was a difference, of course, for though it had been hard waiting to be a martyr, though his martyrdom never materialized, he came to warrant his radical posture, and learned, slowly, to live with imperfection. In Berkeley to stay, still often crude, still monumentally concerned with the progress of his life, confirmed by the many people who never failed to find him overwhelming, he was finally in character, a composite of the many roles he had played, at last somewhat comfortable with the *mélange*, no longer compelled to mark his passage through life by hyperbole, more trusting in himself, for all the anomalies.

When I last saw him he carried off the package with his usual finesse. After all the struggles, he had found a scene and a scenario. The location was Berkeley, among friends who shared enough experiences through time to in fact become a community, and the story line was and would be the endless confrontation of the people—now confirmed in their choices—against the forces of evil.

In the earlier days, when everyone had more to prove, his obvious enjoyment of the perquisites of being a man who burned his draft card had often upset more purist members of the Resistance and those who pledged themselves to the antiwar effort without the trappings of such rhetoric and such blatant personal hungers. Though he dismayed these people, he did take his chances, and he did make his commitment. In time, being only human, he learned, and that, after all, was part of what the revolution was about. More important, despite his colossal shortcomings, he could dream, and did in fact present in words a vision of that new world, a feeling for what could come to pass, far as he himself might forever stand from being the man to see it through.

Cut off from the larger society, fixed enough on the wheel of Berkeley life to be able to have his mail delivered to the Café Mediterraneum, capable of appreciating the humor of his overblown commitment, glad it had not cost him more, he found his place. In the process of playing the revolutionary he had finally come to feel what he had said so many times. Now, with his people, his tribe, he could live with those who shared his view, those whose dreams and fears were very close to his own.

And though he had no good reason for believing that he would fit in that brave new world, though it was conceivable that he would overdress for the day and greet it with an off-color joke, he was in fact and would continue to be genuinely moved by his own cinematic vision of the Second Coming, his reworking of the "Late Show" film in which the captured American fliers march out of the prison camp, heads held high, proud and defiant. In his script, it would be the day when the poor and the crippled, the hippies and the blacks, the Indians and the Mexican-Americans—all the tired and almost beaten—it would be that day when *the people* would, to the sound of some great anthem, march together toward the sunset and that promised land.

· 7 ·
Om

By early 1968 Berkeley politics and Haight-Ashbury styles were spreading rapidly through the country. Campuses everywhere were in turmoil; everyone was getting loaded. Back in Berkeley, where it had all begun, there had already been time to weigh the results of several years of change. Though more stylish radicals now made love with guns under their beds and discussed techniques of making bombs, though freaks still sought converts to the drug life, radical politics had reached an impasse, and the first undertow of the psychedelic rip tide had taken its toll. Unclear about the shape of things to come, Berkeley people were into hustles, or had retreated to safe corners.

It was time for considering alternatives to the chaos that had become part of daily life in Berkeley, so I gathered my gear and headed down to Mexico. I stayed only long enough to find that it was no place to stay. Expatriates sitting in the sun talked of being glad to be out of the states, but fed themselves on gossip and boredom. Those freaks living on the beaches found themselves in a doper's nirvana, but the hair-cutting *Federales* were closing in. Apart from the artisans who sold their handiwork to the tourists, I saw no one who did not find the place too primitive for neo-primitivism, too out of it to be far out.

One night, sitting in a bar trying to get up the energy to leave, I watched the owner of the place don a tuxedo jacket, put on roller skates, and climb onto a small, round table. Motioning to an assistant to dim the house lights, he reached for the microphone, introduced himself, and then, to a flourish by the Beatle-coiffed local rock band, brought on his wife, a portly woman of forty who was dressed as one of the Valkyrie, helmet and horns.

Together they skated around the small table until suddenly he swept her up, holding her by the legs, waving her in the air like a human handkerchief. Receiving the applause of the few patrons, he braked to a stop, set her down, bowed, and announced the finale. As he swung her into the air once again, she placed a match between her teeth, and, as she glided past the table top, she swept down, ignited the match, and came to her feet. That was the act.

Their routine settled my mind. It just wasn't my place; they just weren't my people. I moved out to the street, passed the village square, and met an American who offered me a bag of weed. I rolled a joint, pocketed the bag, and joined him for a party at his place. It was a good party, and I was almost sad to be going, until he came over to ask me to pay for the grass. Stunned, I explained to him that I considered cannabis Mexico's national treasure, that it could not be priced, not in Mexico. That kind of bummer was for the states.

Not of the same mind, apparently, he drew a gun. Thinking it over, I opened the door, pointed to the police barracks below, smiled, and said good night. Violating all protocol for hip tourists in Mexico, I tripped my way back through the town, searching for my house, wandering through the streets for hours. After a night spent contemplating how home was home, no matter how messed up, pondering the toughness of the cockroach, I headed north.

It was always good to come back to Berkeley, always a pleasure to return, no matter how ambiguous previous stays had been, even if to come back was a reversion, a recurrence, or a procrastination of finding where one should really be. At the least it was a comfortable pit stop, though it often tempted one to forget the race. Not without reason was it proposed that Berkeley rename itself La Mancha and secede from the Union. It was a town whose inhabitants were often quixotic, and it had its own culture and expectations, isolated in its comfort and history of turmoil and change both from other academic oases and from the pleasure domes of southern California.

It was good to return, if only to meet those who had come all the way, as far as they could go (always under the shadow of the Golden Gate Bridge), to be with those who shared one's need to have come that far, who had participated in the same set of public, and, in Berkeley, therefore private changes. Or it was good to return for no other reason than to be able to gratify the whims of a food trip in one of the all-night supermarkets kept open for just that purpose.

I wandered through the town, skirting Telegraph Avenue and the epicyclic system of friendships and acquaintances that one could renew just by entering the Mediterraneum Café and sitting there for a day. I moved slowly through the town, tasting its basic contrasts, at once warmed by the sun and chilled by the bay breezes, sheltered by both palm and maple, drifting in that autumnal spring which extended each day until late afternoon when the fog rolled over from Mount Tamalpais, threatening winter.

The anomalous proximities of so many immigrant influences never failed to startle the eye: stamped in the varying strains of architecture were the imprimaturs of the Far East, the Victorian West, and the Los Angeles future. In its many facets and moods the town always spoke for both stability and chaos, for an impatience to be done with the past, a yearning for competing pasts, and plans for differing uses of those pasts.

Hare Krishna, just into town, touted itself as something new, albeit old, and Christian Scientists, praying in a church designed by Maybeck along eastern lines, looked with uneasiness at the lumpenproletariat who talked about the land belonging to the people, or belonging to no one. For a town with so short a life history, most residents of which were only several generations into this land and several years into this region, Berkeley carried an enormous historical freight. Those determined either to bulwark or to undermine what they had inherited from so brief a legacy called on traditions they did not yet own, traditions they adopted all too quickly, to give authority and meaning to their transience. Conservative citizens, academics, students, blacks, and freaks on the block alike looked over their shoulders to sift out and redefine what had preceded them, to arm their impermanence with the wisdom and rectitude of the past, whichever past that was, to somehow give outline to an indefinite future.

One of the more outlandish, if not untypical, immigrants to Berkeley was a young black named Duru. I first met him as I meandered through Berkeley on my return, investigating the vegetation which so threatened to swallow up the houses that one had to have a prepared mind to see habitation in such cultivated wilderness. While checking this out in an otherwise quiet bourgeois neighborhood, I heard some conga drumming coming from one of the buildings, powerfully primitive drumming, urgent yet controlled.

At that time Berkeley had quite a few itinerant musicians, guitarists, bagpipers, harmonica players, and, most forceful, conga drummers, hustlers with strung skins who sat on campus luring women with the not-so-subtle suggestions of their rhythms. But this drumming was different. It was polished and finished, something real in a town where appurtenance often passed for substance. I went in to have a look, and met the musician, Duru.

After we spoke for a while he asked me if I knew Om. Startled by the inflection of his question, I gathered that he meant more than the mantric sound, and asked him if Om were a person. He explained that Om was his teacher, that Om was all-knowing and all-beautiful, that Om made everything happen. Since I seldom felt that I made anything happen, since I knew no one who just then had that kind of confidence, I asked to meet the man.

We entered Om's house to the sound of drumming, and Duru joined two thin black men who were rocking back and forth, palms flying, filling the room with the resonating heartbeats. Behind them, her face full with the rhythms, like a spinnaker in a good breeze, a woman who would once have been called an octoroon nodded me a welcome. Beside her stood a young boy, and in the corner, sitting in full lotus position, a bearded black man of perhaps thirty sat on his dais, writing busily, lifting his head occasionally to smile at the musicians, looking for all the world as if he somehow thought that he made the whole thing happen.

He was draped in a sheet, a toga fresh from the linen department of a five-and-ten-cent store, yet it suited him. He had a huge head, held erect but not rigid, and his face recorded a history of suffering, of compassion learned and earned. His gaze was sad but strong. With just a hint of a smile on his lips, of fine bearing, he gave notice of being master of a house with free entry he did not fear to allow.

I relaxed slowly and was carried away by the sounds. The orgasmic rhythms built and fell, now harsh, now gentle, now imperious, now plaintive. They spoke of love and of the coming of the Day of Judgment, they lamented both friendships never shared and the fallen warriors of Om's army. I was taken on a long sea voyage, inspired to give without limits, buffetted by storms, and brought home, tired, worn, proud of having survived, saddened by my losses, glad to have gone, glad to be home, glad to share the experience.

Slowly, the simultaneously erotic and martial sounds died away, and there was silence. Some long moments later the man on the dais asked me my name, introduced those around him, and then said, "And I am Om." Now I fancied myself well traveled, well used to the side shows of the Berkeley circus, not easily daunted by the bizarre ideas people always seemed to get about themselves. Further, I had learned to accept and even cherish the gamut of postures and costumes that freedom and drugs had made so accessible, but this man went beyond the boundaries of my experience. It was almost normal in those days to see someone present himself as Che, John the Baptist, or Zorro, but never before had I ever met an Om.

Om himself, enjoying my reaction, was more than willing to fill me in, to give me an exegesis of his work. His basic theme was that he was the center of the universe, the immutable center, and that as hub of it all, as the life force, it was his obligation to spread the message: love, cosmic love, love by Om. It was his task to build a group of followers of the life force who were not only to consider the abstract principles of cosmic love, but who were to apply them here, now, in the most carnal fashion. Om was into group sex, in a very religious way.

I listened to his presentation carefully, and he concluded by inviting me to join his group, though he advised that it might be better to wait until he had recruited more female disciples. Although I was relieved not to be proselytized, I was moved by the drumming and by the gentleness of those in the room. I told Om that I was moved, that I was even ready to grant that he had in fact made it all happen, in just that way. Warmed by my admiration, perhaps fatigued by the solicitousness of his disciples, Om motioned them out of the room, and we continued to speak.

It was clear that he welcomed a brief respite from the presence of those who validated his view of himself, that he was not entirely comfortable in the cloister of his sect. He told me how he had come to his work, that he had started calling himself Om as a gag, as a con game, just to see how far it would go. After a while he had actually begun to feel that he was Om. During this period, he recounted, he was incarcerated in a mental hospital where the staff devoted itself to the task of bringing him out of what they considered a delusion. Needless to say, they failed. Exasperated, the head psychiatrist finally told Om that he was crazy.

Om paused in his story, and we both sat there, silent, wrestling with the idea that someone thought Om was crazy. I sat thinking that it had been a long time since I knew what sane was supposed to be, unless it meant staying out of harm's way. So we both sat silent, running the thought through our minds, until our eyes met and we started laughing, crying with laughter, in tears for the idea that some psychiatrist in a looney bin thought that Om was crazy. He might well be, of course, but where was cosmic love in the textbooks?

After another pause, perhaps looking back to that time of travail, that period of testing his faith in himself, Om told me that he had finally found his disciples and come west, landing first in San Francisco, living in Chinatown, and then moving to Berkeley to avoid the impending earthquake. He tried to speak of his realization that as Om he endured great sufferings, carried a great load of human pain on his shoulders. He laughed, sadly, saying that Duru wanted to be Om, that he too wished it could be. Nothing would please him more, since it was of course far better to be the slave than to be the master.

Suddenly, shifting mood, he told me that it was he alone who linked himself to the sun with great copper bands, and drew it out resisting from its cave in the heavens. Where there had been darkness there was, through Om and Om alone, light. He explained to me also that he could make the traffic lights turn green, that Duru had tried it, failed, and received a ticket for jaywalking. We shared a smile both for the brashness of his pupil and for the incongruities of Om's powers. But who was to say? The workings of Om were perhaps beyond the ken of mortals.

Through our conversation, underlying it, was a question which Om finally articulated, in the form of saying that I certainly was courteous to a con man. I thought about that for several moments, and responded by explaining that I too had seen myself in various ways, and that others of course had many views of me also, but that it had never occurred to me, nor to anyone I had ever heard of, to use the name, to be, Om. As far as I knew, I said, he was the only Om.

Poor Om. He had come to call himself and to see himself as Om, still doubted whether he could carry the load of being Om, and was from time to time painfully skeptical of his own motives and abilities. Despite the adulation of his disciples he often wondered if he were not insane or a shyster. And even when sure in his work, he was understandably worn by his task, by the output of energy necessary to maintain the universe. I admired but could not envy his mission.

Finally his disciples returned. It was time for me to go. I thanked Om for his hospitality, and left him seated on the dais, his feet in the woman's lap, his hands in the hands of his disciples, gazing into their eyes. I continued to see him from time to time, watched him gather quite a bevy of ardent young followers, and, even after he moved on, followed his progress in the personal-service columns of the underground press. His messages were always the same, as follows:

Om beyond yoga. Holy copulation of the exceptionally erotic and openminded and openhearted, or for those who want to become so through the Highest Yoga there is, which embraces All of Life itself, given by qualified Om lovers, instructed as Om himself showed them. Om. Write Om.

He seemed to have made it, and I was pleased, for in the face of all the ways people found for selling themselves short, given all the hostility and doubt people were accustomed to unload on one another, it was good to see someone stake out a large, even overwhelming claim for himself, inspire that kind of drumming, and, I am sure, some cosmic loving.

Those were open times in Berkeley, and every kind of kook, weirdo, and lunatic made an appearance, as did the freak in us all. Since there were no limits it was up to the individual to make the assertion, to do his thing. If he cared to reach for the paradigm no one would gainsay him the effort. Freed from the workaday world, setting up our own contexts, we had the entire range of history and flow of time from which to cull our models and our credentials. Sensing too that the gods sprung from the hearts and minds of men, we saw no reason not to find the god in ourselves, to cherish and elevate that potential within us.

If our political impotence had recently been demonstrated, if a frightened society would soon send its worst emissaries our way, if the irresponsibility of our solipsism would soon bring us down, there were nevertheless opportunities for one to be whatever it occurred to him to be, just like that, and one might, like Om, possibly find out who he had always been. And after all, we had been waiting a long time for him, and for that part of ourselves.

· 8 ·
Going
Home

"Did you ever have to finally decide?"

Shortly after I bid Om good-bye, after more than two years of tinkering with toys of my own making, I acknowledged to myself that I still looked over my shoulder to the East Coast. Though the distance seemed greater than ever, I wanted some perspective on the changes I had experienced in Berkeley. Unsure of whether I sought an enema or a transfusion, I wanted to return to my roots. Suddenly, I was there.

By the time I saw familiar faces, I understood my mission. I had come back east, to the land of my childhood, to try to clarify the words *right* and *wrong*. After two years of heading steadily to the Left, I wanted to get closer to the *right*. *Right* —that which is just and good; that which is in conformity with the facts; sound or normal; in good health; that which is appropriate, legitimate, or straight. *Straight*.

That was it. I wanted to do the right thing, to get straight, to straighten myself out, to stop cutting corners, to keep, for a while, to the straight and narrow, to be foursquare. *Wrong*, on the other hand, was what I did not want to be. Erroneous, awry, amiss; crooked, bent, warped; perverted.

I had come to the right place. There, in the land of the Puritans, I stood in the shadow of Bunker Hill, Emerson Hall, and John Hancock Hall, ears open to Boston's curious blend of Puritan hymns and Catholic dirges, trying to feed off the residue of centuries of rectitude and strength, absorbing the order and solidity.

Walking through Harvard Square, I studied the faces of students nurtured by a benevolent society. They had signed their contracts without fear, and, in many cases, unknowingly: play by the rules and we promise you a shot at power and success. The students were trooping back from a football game, full of their image of themselves as liberals, nay, even radicals, but well within the bounds. Those not in tweed chose their garb of alienation carefully. After all, it could always be shed.

Guided by the warm psychology of Harvard's court metaphysician, Erik Erikson, each student armed himself with the knowledge that though he might suffer an identity crisis, it was all part of going through life, that one should endure since there was more to follow, as the particular strains of being young (free, white, and twenty-one) would yield to the continuities and burdens of maturity (Generativity). Erikson himself, after all, had lived his Bohemian years. But here he was, at sixty, a living testament to his gospel that puberty is never over.

The students also had the rectitude of this center of learning on which to draw. Protestant Harvard, sure of what it was not, proud in its postponement of gratification, had been told by a more conservative country that it lay to the left of center, and, like all who believe what they see in such mirrors, accepted this definition without trial by fire, almost gladly, despite demurrers. If any further assurance were needed to accept such stigma, there was always the overwhelming sense of imminent power. Did not the Kennedys and Rockefellers matriculate at Harvard? Did they not sip sherry in these same halls? Was it not former Dean of the College McGeorge Bundy who so influentially guided the course of the war in Vietnam?

I met an old classmate in the square. He deplored, he told me, the trouble in Berkeley. A shame, to be sure, that mindless radicals could jeopardize so fine an institution. Filling me in on the news, he told me that he was soon to go to Vietnam, to plan bombing strategies. Oh, he didn't much like the idea, but he didn't want to risk his career. It was something one had to do.

Then I realized why I had come back. I was to star in a low-budget film entitled "The Return of the Square." In one fell swoop I would end all the anomalies: to hell with politics, such as they were; to hell with Huey, with drugs, with freaks. I would join the circle, the inner sanctum, once more. Bygones would be bygones. I would be judiciously concerned.

Sad to say, I couldn't carry it off. After a visit to Maine, winter closing in, derelict Indians on a postage-stamp reservation, I headed west once more, resolved to enter heaven in saffron robes, all bells and beads, or to move with the Movement to the promised land. I had gone too far to turn back. Fresh photo of my past for the psychic album, I went west to rejoin the people.

· 9 ·
The
Two-Thousand
Million

On the street once again, I bumped into an acquaintance from Telegraph Avenue, a fellow whose every physical characteristic lent him an innocence his actions steadily belied. A check-passer, his *modus operandi* was to register in some junior college, open a student bank account with a minimum of capital, and then cash in on his Midwestern folksiness and ample reservoir of "Yes, sirs" and "No, sirs," to flatter store owners with that much-missed respect from the younger generation while he wrote out checks his meager account was never meant to cover.

Now, however, his game was up. Authentic students, no longer very popular with the working community, too often short of money, were themselves so nearly criminal in the eyes of the larger culture, so much hell were they raising, that they had spoiled his image. Angry at those with so many opportunities who could mess up a good thing for a poor boy like himself, he told me that he planned to look into credit cards.

If things in Berkeley were changing, I had only to visit friends in Richmond to find things more or less the same. Richmond, only miles from Berkeley but in any real sense much closer to Los Angeles, was marked for most of those who circumnavigated the Bay only by its unreal one-hundred-foot oil torches, imposing industrial candles intended simply to expedite business as usual. Otherwise Richmond was no more than the town that happened to have the train tracks and stop lights which slowed travelers to Marin County just before they fused with the suspended grace of the Richmond-San Rafael Bridge.

But behind the award-winning civic center, past the Iron Triangle ghetto area, beyond the car lots, supermarkets, taco stands, drive-in banks, and neon champagne glasses fixed to store-front walls, there was a quiet bar where the same crowd always gathered, where one had the certainty of always hearing the same story,

Fat Frank, the bartender, a heavy-bellied man with a baby face and black goatee, a man who fixed his hair with pomade and was proud of it, was in fact into the superiority of mind over matter. His bulk notwithstanding, it was the intellect he respected. The most notable manifestation of his commitment to reason was his solution to an unending series of paternity suits. Thinking the problem through, he arranged to have his tubes cut, to have a vasectomy. Tasting the benefits of the scientific process each night, Fat Frank knew that brain could only help his brawn have a better time.

Welcoming me back to the bar, pouring me a beer, Frank immediately picked up where he had left off a month before, that is, in his rap about how to build a perfect network for the distribution of speed. The conversation had started late one night in his small modern apartment, which he had decorated like a bar done on Polynesian themes, with palm fronds, co-

coanuts, and bamboo, a strobe light moon high on one wall. The romantic atmosphere that all this produced never failed to impress the girls he brought in for the night to sample his tied-tube potency.

It was in this Richmond beachhead of the South Sea empire that he explained his plans, which, though constantly subject to revision, in essence inhered in a system which was a testament to Jung's theory of the racial unconscious. On his own, in Richmond, California, Fat Frank had come forth with an organization plan for the production and sale of dope in which no one could get burned and in which the bust of any one man would in no way jeopardize the lives of others. In brief, he conjured up the same pyramid of personnel used by the Algerians against the French, a structure in which the members of each subtriangle would know only one other person. At the very top he, and he alone, would know the key figures of each subdivision. Not only would he himself be safe, dealing only through lieutenants, but he would be in a position to freeze cadres out of the organization if they gave him trouble. It was, he argued, foolproof.

Needless to say, such foresight involved a vision of the use of profits. Fat Frank had many ideas, of course, but his favorite was a scheme for a floating bar on Lake Tahoe. He had looked into styrofoam, approved of it, and figured that it was just the substance for the job. Other than that he would need only a gas generator, a chemical toilet, and Christmas lights. Christmas lights? Yeah, Christmas lights, to attract all the boats.

When at last he concluded this particular description of things sure to come, Fat Frank turned as always to give some attention to the house mascot, an old wino named Richie. Each night, for the benefit of the regulars, Richie would tell the sad tale of his latest binge. And always, down in his cups, Richie would cut short the laughter by saying that the government had the obligation to put a roof over his head, that in the United States of America he warranted the wherewithal to live.

Though Fat Frank was condescending toward Richie, he always listened carefully. And always Richie spoke about the Richmond police, about how he had been in jail more than one thousand times. Though he didn't mind going back, since he was old enough to make good money as a "trusty," running paid errands for other prisoners, he had a recurrent dream in which he led a crusade of a thousand winos. With them he would demand a jury trial for every poor drunk, clogging the courts, introducing the concept of due process for winos too.

I stayed in Richmond as long as I could, putting off reentry to Berkeley for a while, but I finally heard the stories one time too many, and headed home. In Mel's Drive-In, open all night, the same two sidewalk psychologists who had been there each night for two years sat waiting for some hippies to come in. Originally their consideration of human affairs had led them to try some controlled experiments. They introduced a stimulus to a social interaction and recorded the results. Over time, however, this interest had become transmuted into a desire for power. Hence they created a game for Mel's Drive-In in which they invited stoned freaks to join them, gradually manipulated the conversation, and culminated the play as one or both sucked the blood from the psychic jugular of some poor tripping fool.

Though vicious, their mind-fucking was not so far from the new norm of things. Even as the local bikers were busy killing each other off while under the influence of a new drug called Angel Dust, other residents of the area were trying to cope with what had proved to be life itself. Peace, love, and sexual liberty, the hopefulness and easy gaming of the bourgeoisie, none of this seemed any more real than a trust in the basic goodness of man's instincts.

The new world was riddled with troubles, yet it was increasingly difficult to relate to the larger society, to conceive of any functional relation to it. We had walked away from that world initially in the thought that it would not be very hard to build our own. Ignorant, we found ourselves in turmoil, yet came no closer to returning to what we considered corrupt. Who knows what gave each person the feeling that nothing from that past world was too dear to give away?

For myself, that feeling is contained in certain images— machine guns on the steps of the Capitol, or, more cinematic, the funeral of Martin Luther King. To the degree that my background gave me a stake in or sympathy toward the larger culture that many of my peers did not share, it was the death of King and his funeral that severed some final connection I had maintained while others moved on.

Already past his peak when cut down, King was buried on a bright, stinkingly hot day. There was a five-mile march, a mule-drawn farm wagon (commandeered from a Hollywood set), and a cavalcade of stars and politicians, all paying off debts and crimes with a pilgrimage in the heat.

Around the prominent, behind the caisson (so the announcer called it, bringing John Kennedy to mind, destroying the imagery the SCLC had chosen for its fallen leader), marchers by the tens of thousands sang the words. We shall overcome, some day. All the resonances of that melody tumbled forth, stronger in this death than in the give-and-take of life. There were, at least, no ambiguities in a funeral. The song was religious, a hymn, the message being that the Lord knew the way of the righteous: the ungodly would perish. But the issue that destroyed the last years of King's life, namely, just how the wicked were to be destroyed, that issue was subsumed in sheer grief, and the mourners let sorrow beg the question.

It was Reverend Mays, weeping, who gave the eulogy and the indictment. No longer tame, he pointed the finger. It didn't need to be said. Before him 150,000 people crossed arms, linked hands, swayed gently, a huge mass with one heart, and sang with a single voice that anthem and prayer: We shall overcome, some day.

White hands, however, were all over the proceedings. In his emptiness the white announcer gave the television audience a play-by-play, lest the vacuum of silent viewing, the experience of sitting quiet with the truth, suck the country in whole and destroy it. Counting the crowd like a sportscaster, giving the temperature, he desecrated the remains. What was left of the man was far more than his corpse, and needed no description.

The empty smoothness of the telecast and commentary, its many cameras and tricks of technology, this sought to measure the flow of feeling by lines on a chart, measuring form but, of course, missing content. In the face of these wonders the nation had produced, in the face of this most explicit statement of a national faith in technology, an old Negro ("I am three-score years and ten and more," he said), an old man who had hoped to have King eulogize him, this old man spoke in heavy cadences, in dated language rife with mispronunciation, and did justice to his pain. He spoke to the memory of a man, to the needs of those who had lost a leader, a dreamer, a warrior.

The eulogist knew, moreover, that he had himself lived past his time, that his sorrow was not simply for the death of one man, but for the passing of the terms of the struggle. Now the battle cry of death was on all sides, and the rapidity of action, the use of media which had need only of image, threatened to make victory, if achieved, a whore's token. It was fitting and proper, then, that an old man, grunting, sweating, and rumbling, the wrong man for this electronic miracle of our land, a man whose time was past, it was fitting that he deliver the eulogy. He had much to mourn, and little to celebrate.

Few of my peers in Berkeley shared my sense of loss. For them King had compromised too much, was too locked into the same old struggles. It was true that he was a politician; it was also true that he could hardly be said to be psychedelicized. Nonetheless, his problems were becoming ours, and his death and funeral closed the past with a finality I had long resisted.

In Berkeley people were learning to say the word *pig*. It took no time at all. But I was leery of the word, and the actions it implied. I was still thinking of Bobby Kennedy on the floor, one eye open, one lid drooping shut, rosary in hand. And I was thinking of Warhol, bullet in his body, finding no place just then for pop art.

In this period too I had reason to remember a card game of a year before. In that game I had met a fellow who called himself Tree Sloth. Indeed, others referred to him simply as Sloth. "Deal, Sloth," they would say. Or, "Do you want to cut, Sloth?," they would ask. It was now some time since the game, and, meeting a friend who had also played, I asked him how Sloth was doing.

I was told that Sloth had been broke, became desperate, went into a liquor store in Los Angeles, begged the owner's pardon, and took ninety dollars from the till. As he reached the door the owner shot and killed him.

So much death in the air, I tried to figure it out. Tree Sloth was no robber. He had no weapon with him. He was, to use the word, a hippy, no more, and no less. It could be argued, I supposed, that his way of life implied such a death. But it seemed to me, just then, that Sloth was simply robbed.

Reacting to what he sensed as a tendency to apostasy on my part during this period, a friend wrote me the following note:

> we are more than turned on. we have started tuning in, to our beautiful bodies and minds, much higher than our straight, uptight, unfortunate counterparts. today, for all our confused, burnt-out brothers and sisters who aren't making it, today, let's stop. let us take care of our own while we try to speed up the higher vibrations of an Aquarian age.

By this point, however, though I felt his kindness, I could barely read the words. The confidence seemed dated, the language remote. We had lost *sophrosyne*, moderation, temperance in the face of a monstrous world. That it was a monstrous world, well, by this point no one could be surprised. The question was still what to do, and it was hardly surprising that in this period many of us looked beyond this world for a new point of vantage.

· 10 ·
Getting
Religion

"You better get a home in that rock, don't you see?"

Tired, thinking about how many houses (if not homes) I had
entered without finding one where I felt I could rest, I accepted an invitation one night to go to a meeting, about which
I was told only that I would see something I had never seen
before. Game, I drove across the Bay Bridge once more, into
San Francisco, past the fairy-tale downtown, past the Hall of
Justice, and coasted down Fell Street into the Haight-Ashbury.

In 1967 I had stumbled into the Haight for the first time,
just in time for the initial Gathering of the Tribes in Golden
Gate Park. Self-consciously mythic though it was, the day was
full of the taste of something new. The petty constrictions of
dying worlds had been cast off, and the infinite lay before us, a

field of fight. Thousands of freaks-to-be stood together, many in costume, sharing food and drugs, chanting "Hare Krishna," listening to the music. That day so many shared feelings—vibrations, they came to be called—conjoined to yield the euphoria of communal baptism. Nothing could hold us from ecstasy. We had been reborn, free: Revolution. Copulation. Liberation. No holds barred.

The day passed all too quickly, and Allen Ginsberg, cymbals on fingers, led the chanting that was to mark the end and a beginning. The sun sank slowly over the trees, a flock of birds winged before it, silhouettes, and the manifesto had been delivered. More jaundiced eyes might have doubted that such a day could be extended, or have noticed that the parachutist who dropped from the heavens of course needed a great deal of technology to carry off his stunt. Nonetheless, that day we were all ready for myth, and no one denied the miraculous.

Soon after, Superspade, a black dope dealer, was dead, murdered, the first clear and notable casualty of life in the Haight-Ashbury. It took some time for the terror to subside and then emerge as the new normality, but it came. Murder, the very word, changed everything.

Though the portents boded ill, no one wanted to confront what was sure to be true. Everyone said that they wanted to slow things down, to step out of that infernally dizzy pace that kept the straight robots going, everyone said that they wanted to feel, to have some quiet, some peace, but somehow the pace was ever faster, speeding more and more, careening out of control. Suddenly it was a foot race, and we were running madly to break clear, to burst that last barrier, but Death lost nary a stride even as he set the tempo.

Each day there was another mind-blowing inversion of what had to that moment seemed the inalterable nature of things, each day a form was resuscitated, revitalized, redefined, rearticulated, reborn, yet simultaneously another set of forces was pulling us down, grinding us down, bringing us to bay. Was it sabotage? Were they out to get us? Who were they? What did they want? Was it us?

Though in time I had learned to avoid the Haight, though I chided myself for coming so close to a scenario of such disappointment, I trusted the judgment of the person who had suggested that I attend the meeting. Parking, entering the hall, I saw a group of several hundred people of various ages and backgrounds seated in folding chairs, listening to a man who seemed to be talking about stars and the relation of stars to each life. Irritated with what seemed to be discussion of games too often played, I moved to leave, and was just at the door when I saw the speaker rush to the forward edge of the assembly. The movement, so abrupt, so violent for the context, startled me, and I stayed to watch.

The speaker, a short bull of a man with a paunch, chunky arms and legs, wide face and a cowl of brushed curly hair, perhaps forty years old, was questioning a man who had just asked him a question. As the exchange progressed the room became quite still, the conversation one-sided, an interrogation conducted by the speaker.

"You ask me what my background is. What do you want?" This was the question put forth by the speaker, each word firm, forceful, direct, his eyes fixed on the man who had asked him for his credentials. Confused, the man tried to adjust to this turnabout. After several interminable moments of silence he began to flush, only to hear a voice in the back of the room repeat the question ("What do you want?"), and remained silent, working within himself for an answer, some answer, unable to discern from the sudden shift in situation or from the intensity of the speaker's voice (as if there had been some grotesque affront) what level of response to offer.

From another corner of the room the question sounded again: "What do you want?" Now he was on his feet, though no one had suggested that he stand, struggling for words, unable to get them out, guests to the meeting now wondering

120

what in God's name they would answer to this question. Just as he seemed ready to answer (or was it simply our hope?), women in long gowns standing throughout the room began to call out the question, strong high voices from every quarter, voice after voice, "What do you want?" "What do you want?" "What do you want?" He turned from voice to voice, staggered by the pace, trying to evaluate the meaning of the question and so formulate some reply.

Then one of the women, sweeping across the room moving rapidly but with control, began to question him.

"What is your name?"

"Jack."

"What did you mean when you asked Alex about his background?"

"I just wanted to know more about him."

"Why?"

"Just to know, that's all."

"What would that give you, that information? What do you want?"

The man stood looking at her, trying to meet her eyes, and finally sat heavily as though she had forced him to the chair, mumbling that he didn't know what to say. The speaker, whose name, I gathered, was Alex, was still standing just inches before those in the front row of chairs, not moving at all, still staring at the man. Time seemed suspended. Everyone in the room waited for him to say something, anything, somehow to give us more information so that we could handle this violation of protocol, this mayhem, given what we had considered the implied contract of such surroundings.

Still staring, the man called Alex abruptly began to laugh, a laugh that started as a series of chuckles and then began to shake his frame, laughter transforming the implacable stare, laughter washing through him and over him, his eyes now twinkling though still fixed, tears on his cheeks, the women in long gowns and various men in the room laughing too.

Though the laughter was deep and its cadences natural, though it seemed without malice, the change in mood was so sudden that the assembly was still quiet. Further, they could not yet fathom what was funny, from what concept of humor this laughter welled. The man who had given his name as Jack watched the speaker apprehensively, a nervous smile now on his lips, too willing to believe that some way out had been found.

All eyes were still on the speaker, waiting for him to give order to this yet stranger turn of events, watching him enjoy what he apparently found so comic. For his part he seemed to sense the very moment at which every person in the room attended his resolution, that instant in which every person present yearned for an answer, for an end to the outrage, and, exercising an unbelievable control, suddenly funneled the laughter into a tight smile, reached the side of the room without seeming to move, and began to talk with the man who had been so unfortunate as to ask him a question, talking at the man, through him, his every word infused with just a trace of irony and deprecation, as though there were some obvious joke he did not expect the man to understand.

"You see, Jack, what the lady wondered was if you possibly thought that we were supposed to put on some show for you, if you entertained the idea that we would perform for you, or that you might listen to our answers and perhaps show us your understanding of life."

The speaker began to laugh again, as if to himself, and then again abruptly channeled his laughter.

"Well you see, my friend, the question has little to do with us. It has, rather, everything to do with you, with what you really want. To tell you the truth, Jack, if you don't know what you want from us then you have no business being here. Do you know what you want?"

The man was silent.

"Are you sure that you don't know, Jack?"

Still he was silent.

"Then why don't you leave, now, and come back, if you want, when you know what you want. Thank you."

It was staggering. With a smile he was telling the man to go, and from the inflection in his voice, the precision and tightness in the last "Thank you," there was no question that the man could stay. The visitor pulled on his coat, looked around the room, and walked out the door.

Overwhelmed by the sequence of surprises, the shifts in mood, the reversals, and the obvious control of the speaker, the assembly sat quiet, trying to gain some perspective on what had just occurred. Even the assumption of familiarity in the use of the man's first name, over and again, was disturbing, as if there were no distance between strangers. Just the disregard of social space was outrageous. And the whole encounter? It had been like witnessing a rape, so intimate was the questioning, so violent the insistence, so intrusive the pressure on what had proved to be so helpless a victim, one of us.

Even as the assembly worked back through the last few minutes in which so much had changed, the man called Alex had returned to his position in the front of the room, and had begun to speak again.

"We are a group that works together to build higher levels of being. We are all crazy, like you. We try to work together to help ourselves. This Work cannot be done alone. Together we attempt to follow the masters. If you do not know what you want from us, do not return. If you think that there is something for you here, there will be another meeting, in this hall, next week at this time. Good night."

With these words he sat down in a chair, back straight, hands on his knees, staring straight ahead, unblinking. Since no one now dared question him, the crowd filed out of the room, the more verbal (males, particularly) quick to dissipate the impact of the events in words, others silent, wending down to the street. As I climbed into my bus I could focus only on the

123

man himself, his clarity, directness, and control, and concede that I had in fact never seen anything like him in my life. True, I had been shocked, but what stayed with me was the intentionality of the effect he had produced, the obviously purposive staging of the whole evening.

Like many others in the room I had more or less presumed that I was to see a show, a spectacle perhaps, that the actors would be more than eager to please, that I would subsume the evening as yet another little taste of life to add to the larger mix, on all of which I alone would pass final judgment. Yet here was this man telling us, showing us, that we could do no such thing, and more, making us silent (and frightened?) accomplices in his pressuring of one of us, his turning of the tables. To cap it all, he had the effrontery to bind us together with him in a union that did not flatter: Like him, he had said, we were all crazy. Oh, it was enormous, and I was much impressed.

In the week which followed I tried to explain to several friends what I had seen, but most of them assumed that I had simply gotten religion, or a little dose of it, like everyone else in Berkeley. It was, to be sure, a common phenomenon in those days to meet someone with whom one had shared a bond only to find that some new cause had restructured their perceptions, that the past was for them subsumed by the categories of the new faith, whether it was drugs, politics, or religion, all enthusiastically espoused, swallowed whole. Generally these commitments passed, and one learned to wait out the cycle.

In any case, religions were booming in Berkeley just then, other modes having failed. In the spate of gurus the jet-setting Maharishi, still in vogue, led the way, appearing with the Beach Boys, the blessing of the Beatles not yet rescinded (though sure and solid Ringo was back from the ashram—he didn't like the food). His Holiness was not helped, however, by a well-publicized photograph catching his overwhelming delight at being given a ride in a helicopter. From a less un-

American front, meanwhile, the moral warriors of the Campus Crusade for Christ had invaded Berkeley, bright-eyed and unsullied salesmen who were pleased to offer a Bible conveniently reduced to four easy-to-read pages.

Aside from these two well-organized faiths, both of which were selling briskly, Berkeley was blessed also with countless swamis, all with fervent bands of acolytes, and the normal number of Haight Street messiahs. Understandably, then, even as yet another instant anchorite passed by on Telegraph Avenue, I had difficulty communicating to anyone that I had seen more than the proverbial light. Moreover, in the process of trying to relate the experience, I only lost hold of it. Irritated, wondering what I had really seen, I resolved to return.

Unwilling to seem like easy game, I came late to the meeting, if only to show the man that I was under no spell, and entered the room, now overflowing, to hear him talking about working. He kept using the word *work*, and for him it seemed to be in capital letters. I could make nothing of it. He spoke also of higher and lower levels, and it all sounded like cult gibberish. Perversely pleased that there was nothing new under the sun, I was just congratulating myself on my perspicacity when the speaker suddenly wheeled toward a woman with a child, stared at her in angry silence for a moment, and then said: "Would you mind taking the baby out of the room? Its crying is disturbing what we are here to do."

So violent was his tone that she gave him a long look of bitterness, and then, as if she feared for the life of the infant, wrapped her shawl around the child and went into an adjoining hall. Changing tone as he watched her leave the room, the speaker resumed his discussion of terms that had no resonances for me, and was just concluding an exegesis of some nuance when the girl returned with her child and sat down. Speaking on for a moment, he then turned to her.

"You probably think that I was wrong to tell you to leave the room, that your child gave you some special privilege not available for others. Let me say this. That is your child, not mine or the child of anyone else here. If you want to stay in this meeting you will have to take care of what is yours. If not, if you cannot handle what is yours that much, then you intrude on what we are trying to do and must go."

She sat there, stunned, her jaw working, and then, bursting into tears, picked up her child and moved to the door. As she reached the threshold he sang out in a very clear, very strong voice: "Thank you very much." The assembly sat silent for a moment, taking in this brutal attack, this unwarranted coercion of a helpless person (a mother with a child!), and then groups of visitors, sure now in their outrage, clear in their unwillingness to witness such bullying, smug with the confirmation of their worst suspicions, picked up their things and in relieved self-righteousness left the hall.

When the room had quieted down once more the speaker resumed his presentation, and, strangely, was even more forceful than before, as if he had gained by having some of those present leave thinking he was a monster, as if he could now speak more directly to those of us who remained, presuming a closer bond between us.

"We are a group doing the Work. Many of our teachings come from George Gurdgieff. We learn also, as he did, from any higher man. We have a ranch, and each weekend we work on the ranch. We have a fourth-way school, that is, not the way of the yogi, the monk, or the fakir, but a school in life, a school to build being. It costs two hundred dollars a month for each person to work, payable in advance. If there is something you want from us you may come, but do so only if you intend to get your money's worth. Otherwise you will only waste your time and ours."

He then said that he would answer any questions, and was immediately asked by a male in hip garb why he was so harsh on people, why he was not more loving. Listening intently to the phrasing of the question, looking steadily at the man until he had finished, the speaker allowed several long moments to pass before responding in a gentle voice that was full of warmth.

"You know, I am sure, that we can all read the words of Christ and other inspired men. Many of us do. Yet after all is read we do not act on these words. We aspire to something finer but do not approach it. Our premise here, then, is that we must first confront the worst in ourselves, our mechanicality, our sleeping state, and then, perhaps, hope to find our way to love. It is of course our being-obligation to care for others. Yet here, now, we cannot, even as we try—we do not know how to begin. With luck, with Work, we will be perhaps no more than part-time killers, liars, cheats, and fools. With the help of others in this Work we may be able to remember ourselves, to work to our finest part, but we can do nothing before confronting, fighting, and accepting what we are now. We begin at the beginning."

His response to the question was in many ways a traditional answer to a traditional proposition. One could take any stand on so large an issue. What was striking about the speaker's response was the overwhelming softness of his words in their simplicity and directness, a softness as extreme as his anger moments before. The longhair, hearing the tone and the message, perhaps himself unsure after preaching love as a way of life, whether or not it was practicable in the form he proposed, nodded and sat down.

Fielding further questions, the speaker then explained where the ranch was located, who Gurdgieff was ("a man who taught the Work, a man of a higher level"), and procedures for meetings. One girl, raising her hand, said that she wanted to join the group, and, picking up on the terminology he had used, said that she wanted to do the Work.

He smiled at her, his eyes engaging hers, and in strong even tones asked her where the money for the group would be found. Quick to reassure, she said that her father gave her money, that she had more than enough to use. Still smiling, the speaker replied that she could not use that money, that she could return only when she had earned the payment herself. Answering the question just forming on her lips, he said: "You probably think that your father owes you something, this money perhaps, or you might even think that he is glad to give it to you and that you should accept. Nonetheless, since the money is no more than a token of payment you cannot render in any other form at this time, you will be unable to invest if the price can be so easily met. From nothing comes nothing. At this time you have nothing to offer. Why don't you go, and come back, if you want, when you have something with which to pay?"

Again those in the assembly were stunned. One could assume, until then at least, if one sought some fault, that the speaker was doing all this for the money. Two hundred dollars a month, per person. The mention of payment had for the moment provided an out. But now, in this move, the speaker had made it appear that there were other concerns, that he had no shortage of applicants, that there were other terms to meet. Even as I realized that it was a good gambit, to turn one away and so attract ten others, I was impressed. If the man were no more than a charlatan, he knew a lot of tricks, and played them consummately. Or he might be, as he said, crazy (though the word seemed for him a definition of mankind rather than a term for aberrants), but he played out his madness with great dexterity. In any case, he had presented more than a simple shell game.

The questioning was terminated, and he then said that those who wanted to join the group would have to decide by a week hence. The meeting would begin promptly at eight. No one would be late. And then, closing the proceedings, he said:

"If you come you will pay me to pay yourselves. If you join us you must get what you want. If you do not, do not stay. There are many other ways. Here we try to get past self-pity, we try not to live in our imaginations, we try to do our being-duty. Here we try to become conscious, to be intentional actors, to choose. We may not succeed. If you come you may wish that you had never heard of this Work. I warn you that we are all lunatics. Good night."

Again I drove across the Bay Bridge, moving smoothly above the water, lulled by the steady procession of lights, easing past the toll booth and off the freeway to home. I kept thinking about his remarkable display of energy and purpose, his overwhelming control and intensity. Though I had met my share of committed individuals, I had never seen anyone whose faith translated so directly into palpable energy, whose beliefs seemed to yield such presence, such authority, such power. He was an incredible force. Though I was wary of being gulled, proud as I was, I was impressed, and I remembered his words about getting what we wanted. Perhaps his motives and ambitions were not the question at all.

He had awakened me in a strange way, with that force and that authority, reminding me of some part of myself I felt occasionally but never seemed able to hold. Hearing him, seeing him, I felt rejuvenated, as though he not only had this force but in fact was offering us a way to tap it. That energy, that directness, that clarity, it was hard to feel and not covet it for oneself. And though he offered no more than an opportunity to struggle, there was an exemplum, in himself, of what was at stake. There was a man.

During the next week I tried to make an inventory of what was going on and where I was vis à vis the flow. Having entered a new world two years before, having learned the various lingos, having experienced what the lingos meant, I had found no larger whole that could sustain itself. Over and again I had been amazed, educated, turned on, but the lessons did not cohere, not in the terms they were offered. Further, something in the progress of those years had made me hunger for a coherence. I was tired of the fragmentation of lives, the separatedness, the everlasting competition, the monoliths and tight dyads that set up such great walls. Though several major efforts at cohesiveness on a large scale had failed, I was left with the idea, and, almost inevitably, with the hunger.

I now knew, I thought, what had to be left behind. Who wanted war, who wanted to hassle, who wanted to compete, who could abide the technological wonders that bombarded potentially sound minds? Who wanted to lose himself in defiance, who wanted a lonely peace? But to stop the war, to get some freedom, to stay alive even quietly, kept implying fights, more strife, in which it became hard to remember what was being affirmed, in which the contamination of combat made even the hopeful resemble their adversaries. Who wanted to struggle with the beast any longer, yet how was one to cut the ties to war without cutting the ties to life? Still and all, it was time to find the way.

As for how to do that, well, I looked for someone to guide me, fallible as I was, someone who still had purpose at a time when people were being burnt out at a prodigious rate. It made good sense to surrender to the terms of a life that considered this one profane, if present, to become a novice once again, to unlearn what only got in the way, to deal with the enemy within oneself and so subordinate the world outside. And though the group promised no easy times, it was all the more attractive for just this reason, since too many panaceas had failed after presuming certain and easy victory. It satisfied to read the task as hard, even violent. Surely that was the way of the world, surely that made the goal worth working for, surely there was something to be won, something beyond all the tribulations of this world, some larger mission to pursue no matter what the price, and to hell with the pagans. Surely this man was someone to emulate. That much was certain.

We had failed to hold the center. Mars, blood red, was on the horizon. It was time to strip oneself naked, to go for broke,

to hurl one's way forward in full acceptance of one's ignorance. Get a new master, get a new man.

In the months that followed I paid my money, cash on the
line, and took my chances. It nearly killed me to hand over
two hundred dollars, since I could think of so many things to
do with the money, though I understood how little pleasure it
would buy. The night I went to join, the man before me first
tried partial payment ("I only have a hundred dollars with
me," he said), then offered a check (postdated, for sure), and,
finding no way to hedge his bet, left. Any ploy I had thought
of long since abused, I paid, wincing even as I fundamentally
shared the speaker's opinion that I had nothing to lose. To
even entertain his proposition made that clear.

Coming to the West from an environment in which everything was rule-bound, tight, high in cost, I had spent two
years learning why life should be looser, that things should be
free. Free food. Free people. Free streets. In this period I had
schooled myself in a loosely defined socialism, humanism, and
anarchism. Hedonism, too. Now I went to school again, to
learn that nothing was for free, that I was owed nothing, that
I could look for no free rides, that I had to do it myself or not
at all, with, of course, the help of some very special friends.
And though it would be hard, I was to have the comforts of
limits beyond limits, mandates quite clear if impossible to at-
tain, and the blessing of being able, nay, compelled, to rise
above the worldly travail that occupied the efforts of others,
to remove myself to another frame, far from the causes in
which so many lives had been mired.

*Between the earth and sky, thought I heard my Savior
cry.*

It began with classes, Alex ringing an invisible bell, sometimes making us dance, sometimes leading us in exercises

("What are you so proud of, you fool, you're just an idiot like the rest of us"), talking, listening, teaching. The Work is to go beyond life, to build being. Chief weakness, when converted, is chief strength. Do your being-duty. Begin with self-remembering. No one is special. Don't live in your imagination. Feed the wolf. Break the recurrence. Measure, don't judge. Choose. Get what you want. Pass false personality to essence. There is no stronger energy than from a man who chooses to do something.

Slowly I began to learn the language; slowly I began to taste the lessons, not simply to hear them or to read them, but to eat them raw. Throughout Alex was the prime force, always a brilliant performer, hungry for a large role, shifting postures, moods, volume, tone, begging, prodding, cajoling, bullying, fighting, trying to make us understand, trying to make us act on our understanding, trying to make us keep up with him. And he was in a hurry.

We were all nothing, worthless. Self-knowledge is the beginning of understanding, and we were ignorant. We had no inner unity, we were reactors, reflexive, a function of every random stimulus that came our way. Yet our effort was the key, the attempt to transform ourselves, this most unwilling flesh, to make the effort honest within our limits, to suffer the humiliation and the pain, to beg to be taught. We were all inferior but equal, all and everything and completely nothing, slaves working to be free. There were, as Alex said, no guarantees, but the imperatives drove us on. We were possessed.

Early in my life in the group, I was telling a story to one of the women as we waited for the next meeting, and while I was in the course of recounting it a big man who had been sitting at the table rose abruptly, gave me an angry glance, and walked away. I fell silent. The woman looked at me for a moment, saw that I did not intend to continue, and started laughing. I stared at her, confused, and finally, still laughing, she spoke. "You probably think that you did something wrong.

How funny. You can't believe for a moment that it was your fault, do you?" I confessed that I had and did. "No," she said, "like us all he is confused. Let him straighten out his problems."

In time he did, coming over to apologize. I didn't know what to make of the whole incident, but from it the man and I teamed up for a while. He was Phil, a huge moose of a man who shuffled through life as the perennial fall guy, the oversized buffoon, the morose giant who constantly implied that he was afraid of his own strength, who had never tested it since a day long ago when he had been made to feel out of proportion. He was easy to read, and I was flush with the opportunity to tell it like it was, he wanted (was obliged) to hear what I had to say, so we spoke. It was, after all, my duty to help him do his Work and so my own, to learn and profit from that part of him which resembled me.

Somehow I still assumed that I was immune from the kind of criticism or simple blunt evaluation that was part of the Work. This criticism (really only description) resembled Synanon or group-therapy techniques in some ways, but here the process was underscored and motivated by a cosmology, a religious frame in didactic form, the goal of which could never be said to have been realized. There was no hiding place. In spite of this I hardly looked for lessons or trouble from Phil. I had him pegged.

As we spoke he listened to what I had to say, and, finally, began to make his points to me. The message was simple: I blamed others for what I did to myself. It was a simple point, to be sure, but I accepted the contract between members of the group and did not throw up a quick defense. I listened, he spoke, and I began to feel in the most painful way how many modes I had devised for avoiding responsibility, how many others there were to blame. As Phil said, I chose to be me, from the very start. That was who I was.

The metaphor most used was that we were stars, that from

the stars we chose a life on earth. Whatever the point of origin, whatever the metaphysic, the idea was staggering. Just when did one become responsible for himself? When did the society, one's parents, friends, economic conditions, the weather, when did all this become secondary to one's own choices? I was done with Freud, the tortured maze-maker, I was done with sociology and its pretensions to explanation, I was worn with political analyses. I was my own man. I always had been.

I knew it was platitudinous, this idea, but I heard it, it made sense. So close is the distance between truth and truism, so hard is it sometimes to see what is just before one. Scales fell from my eyes.

Even as Phil watched me run the idea through my mind, he had another lesson for me, bound up in his discussion of blame and choice. He said that I set myself above others. He knew that I thought that I was quite unlike him. But the Work said that he was, like me, quite lost, and that I, like him, was only a machine, someone so bound up in roles that I had no real sense of myself, perhaps more successful in life's little games, but essentially the same. We resembled each other more, certainly, than we resembled, for example, a dog or a god. It was a bitter pill to swallow, and, fool that he was, he knew that I had it coming.

After these initial exchanges Phil kept an eye out for me, filling me in on protocol. It was on my first night at the ranch, seeing people choose places to sleep, that I mentioned my desire to bed down on a hill so that I would be close to the full moon. Phil had to break the news that in the Work the moon was a blood sucker, a viper, drawing energy from the sun, without vital force of its own, thus nothing to seek out. It did not take me long to see the moon in a new light.

The next morning I labored with Phil in the vineyards, watering the plants, clearing the fields for more crops. It was a wonderful day, and I was pleased with the effort and companionship in the task. The day included a sequence out of *Shane*,—getting that giant stump. When we finally triumphed, huge roots beside a gaping hole, a young boy who had been watching (the children of group members also came up to the ranch) came over to us. "You probably think," he said to me, "that your task was to pull the stump. It wasn't at all. It's how you do, not what you do. You were just a fairly good machine. That's not the Work." Phil just sat silent, sweating and smiling.

Though the taste of the day had been taken away, a good meal in the company of the hundred other members of the group and a swim with naked others in the pool left me with the feeling that there was time to figure everything out. The weekend was over, and it was time to return to life, to feed that part of ourselves that lived in the world below.

At the next meeting, in San Francisco, Alex gave us a parable, a Sufi story. A man lay dying of thirst in the desert. A rider came by, on horseback, and the dying man called for water. The rider swung at and struck him with a stick. "No, you don't understand," the beaten man cried, "I need water." Again the rider hit him. Nearly dead, the man begged for water once more, and again the rider hit him, but this time a snake came from the man's mouth.

As always, the parable was a preface for group work. Through group criticism, through the Zen technique of shock through shifting levels, through the didactic precepts, Alex was out to have us, and himself, get past the snake in ourselves. There was the wolf in us, too, which had to be fed so that it would curl up and lie by the fire, but this night Alex was on a snake hunt.

Mike spoke first after Alex finished, telling us how hard he found it to live in the world and still do the Work. Group members listened, sometimes saying something, Mike rambling

135

on, open-faced, head stiff, proper, clean, a straight arrow, persistent in his complaint that he was too pure for a world like ours.

As he was talking Alex interrupted to ask Mike where he was from. He said, "Brooklyn." "You don't say," Alex replied. "Well then, why don't you go back to Brooklyn and be one of the boys for a while, check out the action, if you know what I mean, cut those apron strings." Alex said all this with a leer, coarsely, smiling as Mike drew back from so crude a suggestion. Still smiling, in no hurry to resolve the implied threat (that Mike go back to Brooklyn, that is, leave the group), Alex handed Mike a cigar. There was no choice. Mike started puffing.

I remembered that weeks before, Mike had said that he came to the group to find enlightenment, satori. Alex had only rolled his eyes. Now Mike was going to have to give up that holier-than-thou pose if he wanted to stay. Always willing to undercut pomposity, quick to spot those who wrote off life's little sins too easily, ever ready to shock with profanity or a poke in the ribs, Alex allowed no sanctimony in the group. Holiness would have to be earned, the lessons often beginning with learning to play life to better advantage. Renunciation was not the goal, not, in any case, abnegation by those who sought to foreswear what they had not tasted.

Mike busy with his new form of prayer, Alex asked what else we had to say. Joe, a man of about thirty-five, a school teacher, said that the presence of new members made him uncomfortable. Impatient, Alex told him to say what was on his mind. Joe's story was about life in the church.

"I was in a monastery, you see, and there were of course no women, and we did a lot of unnatural things."

By now Joe was in the center of the circle, and a woman told him to continue, to get to the point (*much laughter*).

"So in the monastery we had sexual desires and we sinned.

136

Brothers fornicated with brothers, and I myself went to the sheep and goats."

The secret told, Joe stood waiting for some reaction. Though it was not unusual for group members to react to what another member said, no one in the group had a feeling for how to respond to Joe's confession. It was Alex, laughing, who had the answer.

"Jesus, Joe," he said, "if screwing sheep and goats is what you want, then how can we help you get more?"

Joe stood silent.

"But I tell you, Joe, if you really want my advice, I suggest you try some cows. Women, moo for the gentleman."

The women mooed.

"You see, Joe, you've got a herd right here. Give them a chance. And in any case, tell me, Joe, do you wear shoes that fit? Get the idea? Think it over."

And then, perfectly mimicking Joe's troubled voice, he said over and again, between laughs, "sheep and goats, sheep and goats, sheep and goats."

Joe, however, was not easily relieved of his sins, and remained certain that there was much more to say about his monastic misadventures. He continued with stories about how celibacy led to promiscuity until one of the men in the group told Joe that he was never celibate, that he was constantly fornicating, in this case getting the pleasure of making us listen to his stories while he brought himself to a climax with the telling.

And then Alex was right in front of Joe, telling him to say something honest, just one clean word. Joe faltered, and Alex hit him hard with one quick punch to the heart, slapped him backhand across the face, and said: "Joe, straighten up or get out."

We all sat silent, feeling the blows, for even beautiful people like ourselves were not so unlike Joe. Even we had our snake,

137

even we tried to turn a profit on our nightmares by seeking company in our humiliation. So it was from Joe, that lowly creature, that we were to learn. In the symphony that Alex conducted there was a need for Joe's sound too. But not for long. He was only an exemplum. There was no time for self-pity, there was no time for unnecessary suffering, for those who were determined to make the worst of the worst. As Alex said, every stick had two handles, and it was up to the individual to chose which one he would hold. No interest here in the specifics of the neurosis. Just a feeling that every problem was simply another manifestation of ignorance, nothing to linger on except as a point from which to proceed. How could anyone identify with actions so absurd? It was, in any case, Joe's choice whether to let this part speak for his whole or not. He had only to decide where he chose to live.

As I prepared to leave that night Alex called me over and asked me, in a casual voice, why I wore corduroy levis and denim shirts. I replied that I found them cheap and comfortable. Smiling—a little smugly, I thought—he asked me to wear a suit to the next meeting. I said that I would. Years of wearing coat and tie behind me, I wondered if he thought that I would find the assignment difficult.

Busy through the week, I put his request out of my mind until the appointed night. Just as I was about to leave the house I remembered, searched in my closet, pulled out a suit, found an only slightly wrinkled shirt, had to settle for socks that did not match, and ran a rag over shoes that badly needed shining. The tie was beautiful. All in all, it had been a long time since I had worn this kind of costume, and I felt pretty snazzy. Nothing to it. At the end of the meeting Alex came over, looked at me, asked me to turn around, and, when I had completed the pirouette, said: "I assume that you know your pants are ripped in back, along the crotch—I suggest that you do your Work tasks more carefully."

My life in the group progressed in much this fashion, a

steady certainty on my part that such incidents were not my norm, and a constant stream of exemplums to show me why I was wrong. As time passed it became increasingly difficult to function as before during the five days each week in the world below. At the very least, the concerns of my friends no longer seemed so vital. What political changes were coming down, what apartment someone found, what films were playing, who was with whom, none of this resonated as before.

Similarly, the way people matter-of-factly spoke of themselves as a whole, as one single responsible entity, no longer made sense. It had taken hold on me, from the group, that people had many different parts of themselves, that each part had its say, that it was obviously ludicrous to try to justify a given part of oneself with one's whole being. My friends, however, whether they did something well or made an error, insisted on taking full credit or blame, whichever seemed appropriate. They alternated between vanity and self-pity.

In any case, I was busy with one set of people, and a new vocabulary and set of resonances. Beyond this, the group had as a postulate that one had to become an intentional actor, and was to begin this by the process of self-remembering, that is, by an impartial review of one's life each day as if seeing a film, and to move from that overview to a choice about what to encourage and what to deny. This self-consciousness, this remembering of self, set me apart from my friends, most of whom were simply running at breakneck speed, and made conversation and friendship ever more difficult.

Meanwhile life in the group had a lot to recommend it. A huge sailing boat had been purchased, and the group now had a new vehicle for the Work. In terms only of the chance to work on a boat (feed the wolf) I was pleased, and as a metaphor the boat carried good feelings. We had found our vessel. In time the boat proved to be full of holes, and the group had to give it up (the boat later sank, owner aboard). But I was impressed with the capacity of the group to engage in such grand projects, whatever higher purpose was intended, and was moved with the collective enthusiasm and energy.

Though the boat passed out of our hands, we had to live with the inevitable lesson. As Alex said, we had been too greedy, too piggish, and had destroyed the purity of the boat. If we learned from the loss, one thing also was salvaged from our experience with the boat. A group member who had fallen overboard had been rescued from certain drowning by other men in the group. Speaking later about the incident, Alex asked the man if he did not agree that he was the type who always fell overboard and drowned. The man nodded, and was in fact someone who was forever sending out distress signals before recurrent calamities. This time, however, he had been saved, with the help of those in the Work. The circle had been broken, he had ended the recurrence, and, if he were willing to do the Work, he could go on, he could ascend to and commence Work in a higher octave. He was free to progress.

The idea of recurrence was one of the primary concepts of the Work, describing as it did the hopelessness of human beings who forever found themselves in more or less the same situation, again the same trap, the faces and time changed, the essentials similar. It was the plight of those forever asleep, those who identified with roles that had nothing to do with their essence, those who were unconscious. If one was willing to pay he had the possibility of making changes in his being. The price, however, could be high. Ouspensky, for example, Gurdgieff's Boswell, provided volumes of exegesis of Gurdgieff's Work, yet would not yield his intellectual stance, whatever the subject and verse of his writings. As much as he spoke of the Work, he perhaps never surrendered the more fundamental posture, his scholasticism, and so missed the essence.

We in the group were bent on breaking the recurrence, and Alex enjoined us to be prepared to pay. As if to mark the end of a stage in our collective effort, open meetings to recruit new members were no longer held. Perhaps Alex felt that there was now enough money each month for our projects, perhaps he had decided that he could now count on a cadre that would survive the tests to come. In any case, the group was now closed, and Alex began to accelerate the pace of commitment.

We were told to study the Book of Exodus, and it was clear that Alex saw himself as a Moses, for the present gathering the people who would wander with him in the wilderness. Each weekend on the ranch he read aloud from Gurdgieff, one hundred and more of us sitting on the ground before him, sky clear, stars above, poplar trees bending in the wind, Alex giving each word full force.

In the same period he announced a redefinition of his own role. He was no longer a group leader—he was a Teacher of the Work, like Gurdgieff. He had new responsibilities to us, and we to him. He needed us, he said, but only those of us who were really prepared to do the Work. It was a kind of spiritual trading, in which we were to give him a certain material that he would use and transmute, he in turn providing us with a good return on our investment so that we also could progress, and on we would go. We were told that the Work would be more difficult, and given time to gauge our desires. At one meeting, taking a reading of our determination, he asked if we were ready to join him. Hands went up around the circle, person after person testifying to a desire to push ahead, whatever the price. Some were still silent.

Though Alex did not press the issue just then, it was becoming clear that whether or not the teachings spoke of the Work as a fourth way, with its disciples living in the world, the group and its Work was becoming a full-time occupation. Not only were there meetings during the week, but extra tasks were assigned, beyond the general effort one was to make each day by himself. Moreover, the stress on the idea that each individual was a lunatic, without intentionality or consciousness, made it increasingly difficult to relate to those who were, by definition, profane. Contact with those outside the group implied a constant double-entendre on my part that I could not sustain. A time of choice was approaching.

As Alex said, one could not sit between two stools. He himself knew what he wanted, and had set out to be a man of Gurdgieff's level. He sought the consciousness of Christ, that member of a school which deliberately created the first Passion play to shock mankind into awareness. He too would present a Passion play, and each of us, if successful, would choose a role. Slowly, as I read the teachings of Gurdgieff, as I read accounts of life with Gurdgieff, as Alex taught, I began to have some small inkling of what was at stake. It was so simple. We were asleep. Could we but awake we would be alive, truly alive. We were puppets, controlled in each moment by external forces which were or might as well be random. The question was how to become masters of our lives, the vision a promise of what might be.

And Alex, taking our energy, promising to do something with it and give us something back, to help us stop being the victims of ourselves? Ah, he was a man both pious and crude, active yet thoughtful, scornful and kind, tyrannical and gentle, public and secretive, a man urgent to get something perhaps unrealizable, a person made of this earth yet most ambitious for his soul, a man who sought the power to be. With us he lived in an atmosphere nearly despairing, at the same time endowed with boundless energy for the struggle.

Hence the haste, the iconoclasm, the search for essence and mockery for appearances, the shocks, the imperatives. How else break himself and us from the habits that left one only half-alive? Hence the pain of those trying to awaken. Hence the disdain, for if others were machines, how not to use them as such? Hence the evasiveness, the contradictions, the jokes, the contempt, the exhilaration. I try to imagine what must have been in his mind as he looked over us, searching for those who might possibly have the courage and grace to build a soul.

What images I have of that time. Alex in a Jaguar XKE, and why not? Or Alex listening as a woman spoke of her joy of what she so briefly glimpsed and to which she aspired. Or Alex fighting with us to the death, for it was in his world a question of nothing less, and that was certain.

In this period Phil left the group. He could not hold a job to earn the money for his next payment. More power to him in his weakness, he did not try to beg a place or avoid the member of the group who kept the books. He simply did not show up one day, and I realized what pain and confusion he was tasting. For the experience could be shared only by those in the group—there was no translation possible. Alex had forbidden us, after a certain point, to speak about the Work to those outside it. The enjoinder was not devised to keep them from us, but rather to enable us to hold to ourselves what little we had. For Phil it must have been hell, wanting to return, not wanting to return, sitting in cafés, watching people pass, living now already with memories, still unable to bring himself to get another job, watching himself lose each moment he had spent, perhaps getting into a conversation, coming to the subject of his malaise, and trying to explain to someone, anyone, what he had been part of.

For seekers still in the group the pace increased again, and now it was clear that there was no place for those who did not subordinate all else to their Work tasks. One night, dealing with one of the married couples in the group, Alex asked the husband what he most wanted. "To be free of my wife," he responded. "Then go," Alex replied, "and come back to us when you are ready." After he left Alex turned to his wife and asked her what she thought. She was pleased, she said. Nodding, Alex asked her what she was going to do now that she was free of the man who had tied her down, for whom she had given up so much. Well, she had to care for the children.

For the next hour and more, group members argued with her, trying to bring her to the point of accepting responsibility for herself. Where was she to get money? From her husband. No, Alex said, she would have to provide for herself. But she could not work, she said, since she was busy caring for the children. And the children? Yes, they were of school age, but she could not entrust them to a sitter, even for a few hours a day.

So it went, group members arguing with her, striving to have her understand that she used the children as an excuse, as she had used her husband, that she was now on her own and would have to care for herself. Still she resisted, backing away, dodging, side-stepping, throwing up the most paltry excuses. It was monstrous, it was foul, but we saw ourselves in her, and fought all the harder to make her come clean, the pace of our collective struggle ever more rapid.

Finally, at just the point when it seemed that she would have to open her eyes, that there was no place left to hide, she said that she could not begin to work until her cousin came. And that cousin? Of course, someone she had not seen for years, about whom she cared very little.

No time left to waste, perhaps concerned that we might identify with her, Alex stepped into the circle and grabbed her by the wrist. She pulled away. He held her tight and, with the greatest deliberation, hit her very hard, once, and then again. She screamed, she cried, and in a delirium of vitriol, pain, and outrage, she ranted of her father and the man who, years before, had told her how much she resembled the Virgin Mary. And then, with a great effort, she broke loose, ran to and crashed through the glass door, and stumbled to the street, calling for help.

Two men started to go after her, but as they rose Alex said, "Stop!" They froze, we all froze, and, as we held the positions of the moment of that call, Alex ordered us to do our Work.

We did, even as her sobs and cries reached the room from the street below.

The next weekend Alex predicted that the group would soon be smaller. Some took it as a new standard, but most understood that Alex was only preparing to realize what had been developing since we began. After dinner that night the men and women met separately, and as we spoke I could hear the women singing, in high thin voices, "May the Circle Be Unbroken." Fear and excitement ran high, and one man presented to us his proposal that we undertake the building of racecars to replace the boat. In a year, he said, we could have the finest racing team in the world. We knew we could, just as we knew that our collective purpose and energy could bring us to whatever vehicle we chose to carry our mission. Though his proposal was set aside, he spoke well for our feeling that in the Work no task in life was impossible.

In this period I, like the other members of the group, had been weighing my future with the group. Like the others I had been taken by the struggle, and I had been moved by the efforts of others who shared the same energy and directness. Like the others, I believed that Alex was a Teacher, a man whose equal I would not see again. Like the others I had a vision of doing the Work with him, to the end, to whatever end.

At the same time, I yearned for the world below, for its sloppy comforts, for its confusion, for its quick rewards, for its very mechanical humanity. Remote, it was even more attractive. Further, I had read about Gurdgieff's school, autobiographical accounts of those who were his pupils, and felt how dangerous their search had been, how risky their endeavor, how lost they were when he died. I knew too his last words to them: "What a fine mess I leave you in."

I did not feel up to the Work, I did not feel I could do the Work, I had come too late, or too soon, or, it just was not to be, not then. I wanted to *be*, for sure, but I also wanted to let things be. I could not give up the world below. There was too much to try, and I harbored the thought that I could always return to the Work at the right time and place. I knew also that I could do no such thing.

I went to Alex and told him that I was going away for a while. I could not bear to phrase it more strongly. He looked at me without surprise and said: "You will not come back." He knew that I understood that he was not stopping me; he was simply telling the truth.

So I left this man, this Teacher, this person who struggled so hard to earn his godhead. A magician, a magus, he was the modern man, working with timeless teachings long after the continuities had been broken. I had little idea of his background, I never learned his credentials, but I believe that his search was honest. Or, if it was not, he in any case gave me some understanding of what it meant to be that kind of man; I got my money's worth. As for his endeavor, I had the feeling that his impatience, his drivenness, his near despair, derived from more than the impossible terms of the Work. It was perhaps the understanding of a man who realized that he might corrupt the vital teachings to which he aspired, or, so few were his guides, that he might create the opposite of what he sought, so finely drawn was the line between success and failure in that fourth dimension he sought to enter.

It was not at all that he was Faust. It was simply that each period of time has a character, like each man. In these times, only fragments of the teachings to be found, only teachers who were themselves no longer sure if their preparation was adequate, even Alex understood his recklessness. But he wanted to be free. Who can judge him?

So I left the group and descended to Berkeley, there to re-join God's plenty. People asked where I had gone, I gave them answers, and soon lost the taste of what had been. They had many opinions. Oh, they had heard about the group, about how it destroyed people, how it made slaves of them, how the leader was out to use them and get rich, how he was a force of darkness, Satan incarnate, a charlatan, a con man, a shrewd manipulator, a fool, the anti-Christ. I responded quietly to them that I had got my money's worth, they did not hear my words, nor did they stop to remember that he who speaks does not know, that he who knows does not speak.

Perhaps Alex stood a chance, if no more than a chance, of becoming a man of a higher level, of reshaping his most fallible flesh. If he sought Christ, I had turned to Chaucer, and that was my choice. Though I prided myself on being tough, I was not tough enough for the Work, and sought the path of the heart through ways I thought I could handle.

To remind myself of another level even as I began to speak of this one, I took the name Beelzebub from Gurdgieff (one of his books was entitled *All and Everything: Beelzebub's Tales to His Grandson*). Perhaps what I had in mind was Gurdgieff himself in Paris, an old man, approaching his death, knowing already that his time was past, knowing too that men would have to live in this most imperfect world, very bad luck indeed having precluded the emergence of a better one, if only for the time being.

In the period of transition I heard Alex's voice over and again: "You will wish you had never heard of this Work." And then I passed out of his reach, I rejoined the rhythms and melodies of the larger flow, and hurried to have my share of the vanities, foibles, whims, conceits, caprices, hopes, dreams, illusions, and insistent mortality of those who could live no other way.

No, nothing was for free. Yes, I would pay. But I would stay with the groundlings, spared perhaps, perhaps not, from that overriding ambition which made such redoubtable prisoners of those who tried the Work. With a confidence born of ignorance I chose to make my own way. And, for so many reasons, some very good and some quite bad, I faced the old religious question and decided that we all, willy-nilly, have a soul, no matter what we try to do to it, and that there are many paths to the spirit immanent in us. I had begun to feel that it was the process of living that alone redeemed us.

In any case, home again, I had seen a man whose existence I would have doubted, a mission I would not have believed. Nothing to write home about, really, but a life and cause that would linger with me as I rode the waves of the Berkeley sea.

· 11 ·
Jason

Jason, a black man who recurrently escaped only to the periphery of the ghetto, surfaced in Berkeley out of the vortex of the late-fifties San Francisco cool scene. For several years, between Beat and beaten people, he lived with and marketed the blues as the black hipster with the rags, pads, and Cads, with the dogs, the shades, and the white broads. Raised in the deep South, he had followed the North Star into the Navy and had seen the world. On his return to the states he had stopped in San Francisco and sent post cards home. He thought he had come a long way.

He established a name for himself between North Beach and the Fillmore, served as a liaison between black and white Negroes, and hustled well enough to enjoy the sound of silver in his pockets. Buying drinks for the boys, accommodating a lonesome woman, everybody's friend, he began to be able to afford *noblesse oblige*. With sweet success, however, he ventured to run a bar a little too far into the ghetto for him to maintain his distance, picked up a misdemeanor, and logged the next year in the county jail listening to traffic roar down the Bayshore Freeway.

Jason learned early how to relate to whites, the available games to play, and his stutter testified to the distance he found it wise to put between thought and action. It was his steady desire to carve out some life space for himself, to somehow turn to advantage the liabilities of ghetto life, that brought him across the Bay to a community in which if anyone were to play the role of heavy, it would be he. Yet above all Jason wanted life mellow, and around the fun and games of the young whites busy becoming *déclassé* he sought to make the best of a bad thing, to get somewhat freer of the tensions and chaos he had grown tired of handling with such careful equanimity.

With drowsy cocaine eyes, a growing paunch, balding slightly, he came on with a smile, open-faced with a half-lidded gaze that missed nothing. He was aware of his status as someone who was "together," a quality attributed to anyone old enough to have been through some changes, to have paid his dues, who could make some sense of the lessons to be learned. Someone was together if he had had time to define himself, to judge himself, to be what he said he was, and to have made an accommodation with the fact. To white hippies going through an endless puberty, still straight-arming what they had been, Jason seemed like the real thing. He had arrived.

In fact he had arrived, but knew too, unlike those who thought only they were forever in the process of becoming, that authenticity was no sanctuary. One did arrive, but only to an understanding that wisdom spoke best to what had been, and counseled acceptance for the future. Jason knew all too well that it was impossible to make repeated redefinitions of oneself, that a man found himself unwilling to give up what he knew best, determined to realize some profit from even the worst investment, if only from the consolation of familiarity.

From his fatigue Jason had learned fatalism, from which he derived an enforced calm in the face of unrealizable hopes. He concluded that freedom of choice was in the way one lived within limits he had not chosen. Freedom was in not feeling compelled to apologize for being alive or for being hungry. One arrived only to learn that nothing was easy, that one worked for what he had. The room for integrity was in the form of accommodation to the inevitable distance between what a person wanted and what he could reasonably expect to get.

It was always Jason's pleasure, therefore, to run with others who were his peers insofar as they shared with him a certain quality of approach to life. One measured not so much what a man did but how he did it. Perhaps Jason learned his lesson early, living in an environment in which all options had high costs. Since, obviously, nothing in the ghetto was for free, one saw the prices for playing white games as well as the penalties for the quick pay-offs of pimping, hustling, or whoring. Each person took his stance and chance. Choice was in how a person ran his death trip. With what integrity to the paradigm. It took class to do anything right, without asking for guarantees that did not exist, without calling for help that was not forthcoming.

Uncles and aunts, mothers and absent fathers could all see the choices coming for a child a long way off. The available postures and roles were both finite and stylized, so it didn't take much guessing. As they figured, Jason, always loath to fight, always hoping for some kind of reconciliation, became an easygoing hustler, quite honest in his fashion, not only because it was profitable, but because running games on people cost him too much tension.

So he lived among the white hippies, hustling a little, teaching the kids the lingo, smoking all that free dope, often be-mused at being asked to explain to them what they would learn soon enough. Generally steady, watching the young whites begin to realize the enormity of the steps they were taking, he would occasionally go on power trips, tempted to domineer or to fleece the innocents. But usually he came on as he was, that is, honest, likeable, eager to be of service, and in-terested in magic.

He spent his days as an observer of the movements of the more reckless and more driven, amicable host to the ambitious when they slowed down long enough to talk about the race. People trusted and confided in him, would occasionally help him out, and invited him to all the parties celebrating their success. With the good friends he so valued, past having to compete with them, Jason found his niche. Black but not too black, old enough to have the Negro wisdom the hippies so valued, he gave up the fine cars for a '53 Chevy with no back seats, kept the two Great Danes, and picked up Ann.

Both Ann and the dogs he brought with him from the fif-ties. He had once used the dogs for status, but now simply loved them, and no longer needed them to enhance his image. It was always a question, however, whether he made the tran-sition with his white woman.

Oh, he dug blowing her father's mind and all, being black and all, with that earring, the leather stetson, the vest, and those boots. Of course he dug the humor and the insult, but he also loved the girl, and didn't like being her blackjack in the family scuffles, didn't like what kept her working steadily for higher degrees, biking daily up to campus, while she lived with him on the flats below San Pablo Avenue. Nor did he al-ways like that part of himself that loved her, or that resented her options.

Perhaps he had simply seen enough to understand what she barely perceived or would not admit, that he would really stay below San Pablo Avenue, despite the dreams, and that she would leave, without him, despite all her hatred of that prep school and suburban Connecticut scene from which she came. For Ann was always quite refined, notwithstanding the rotten house, the broken car, and the lack of money.

Though she thought she kept the secret to herself, she nonetheless manifested her breeding in the lines of her face, the texture of her skin, her silence, and the ferret eyes which took in and appraised everything around her. She always seemed capable of blowing it one day and sitting down at the old upright piano on which so many stoned hippies had banged and coming out with a Chopin sonata. On Jason, himself no slouch, dedicated to an informal but full-time study of his species, none of this was lost.

This is not to say that Jason and Ann did not love each other as joyfully and as desperately as people love. It is simply to say that his inability and unwillingness to leave such congenial misery, his knowledge that the hip scene brought no upward mobility, that outside the hip ghetto he was just another impoverished black ex-con eligible for welfare and warehouse work, that a woman was no ticket out of the ghetto for a man with self-respect, all this was impossible to avoid. Also inescapable was her memory of and revanchist expatriate ambition for that linen, that crystal, and her knowledge that it was still accessible, not yet beyond reach. It was these knowns that undercut and mocked what they had together, day by day.

These two lines of thought, of knowledge, of belief, ran parallel to their love, might have run parallel forever, but instead seemed sure to merge on the foreseeable horizon, the two lines approaching closer and closer together, not only merging but crossing, double crossing, and so confuting each other that in the end love would yield to the possibilities of the future. Nor did this relate specifically to the young hippy chicks he brought to the house, or to her trip home to think it over, these blows they threw at each other.

Do you see where Jason stood? He knew that Billy would

kill himself, that Suede Johnny would hustle and make it in style, that Danny would limp from kick to fix, overdrawing the trust and honesty in his account; but Jason settled for watching it all, his judgment being that these were his people, that this was where he lived. Give it up? How? To go where? To be what? He had learned his limits and was tired of denying them.

So he would walk up to the pay phone on San Pablo Avenue, past the restaurant where Berkeley professors ate gourmet meals, past the Chinese grocer who always beat him for a nickel on each dollar (Jason knowing too that one night someone would take the nickels back, filling the place with flames that would cast their light behind the $1.89 Halloween skeletons that hung in the window). He would walk to the pay phone, make a connection, and spend a day or two or three hassling a deal, traveling with the dogs, rattling off on an empty tank to cross the Bay.

Or he would sit in the local head shop rapping, warning Jack not to make the sale, watching Jack sell three times to the man and take his fall. He'd listen to Rita work her curses, to Cindy describe what kind of man she really wanted, or admire how skillfully Ken slid through the doper's vendettas to make some money. Or he'd watch Johnny in action, taking in how Johnny picked up on a new girl, knowing that a week later she'd be back, complaining about how it was impossible to be one of three wives, Jason understanding as she said the words that Johnny was a king, that he deserved no less. He'd watch the changes, drink some wine, give some advice that no one would follow, and then he'd stroll over to the root-beer stand, busy in his milieu.

Later he would go home to watch Ann dress up for a night at the Fillmore Ballroom, to study her as she got into the Roaring Twenties costume which exposed to advantage the large nipples of her small breasts. He would watch her, fighting his fear that she would go, harder on her because of it.

154

And occasionally he would return in the dying car to the condemned house to look at her and to look at her and to finally rush out of his chair to slap her, to hit her, to take a swipe at her future. Then to make love with her.

Like any two people whose love embodies such contrasts, each argued with himself and the other for possession of rectitude, softness, and tears. Or perhaps, closing off alternatives that seemed hers alone, Ann said a final no to the history of southern Greece, and Jason, in response, stopped snorting the cocaine which promised a life too high and too brief to allow the intrusion of pain.

Jason did no less than to see it all. His Indian, Mexican, and African blood conjoined to give him all the sight he needed and some he did not. He tinkered with the stars, ran through the catalogue of signs, only to marvel at the various ways in which one was powerless. He did not choose to be Jason.

But then again, what friends he had, what love he shared, and what a joy it was to walk the dogs. To know that Ann was a fine as well as white woman, that she knew him to be a man as well as her black lover, that both because of and in spite of their knowledge of each other's bloodlines, history, and pedigrees, they still chose to mate. That she knew Jason to be strong in defeat, presiding over the wreckage, commenting on it, smiling with it, hating it, making toasts to the losses and occasional victories that marked the higher education of those he knew. That she watched him witness the meteors of his time burning themselves out, offering some care when he could.

Look with me now and see Jason on the farm in Alabama, hand-me-down coat and bowler hat, standing with his brothers before the wooden church. Or see him in the navy, dress whites and sailor's cap, arm on the shoulder of a white friend. Or see Jason in a zoot suit, at the bar, girls on either side, or walking into the sunlight after a year in jail. And see him on the street, earring and stetson, whistling to the dogs, calling to them, "Hey Ulysses, hey Regina." Or see Jason sitting at the kitchen table, cleaning the weed, passing a joint, safe from change in the timelessness of his high.

And Ann, see her in a prep-school photo, bitterly composed, scholar in cap and gown. Or bicycling up to campus through the ghetto, pedaling toward what she never left. And see her spread her legs open to the love she so desired, struggling to take the seed for a child not destined to be born. Or see Ann vamping in high-laced shoes, low-cut blouse, and flapper dress, smiling with sharp eyes at the shadows of the future.

They make a pair. Their stars confirm the rutting and the spats, the love and the fear. They stay or part to follow what directs them more urgently than the crazy proximities of those years.

· 12 ·
Big Sur

During those years I often drove down to Big Sur, camping on
the beaches, accepting the hospitality of the freaks who carved
out homesites in the woods and built shacks to survive the
long rain winters. Each summer the Sur was invaded by tourists who kodaked the coast in one grand day. Fresh from the
gingerbread motels of Carmel, or spun out of the whirlpools of
southern California, they negotiated the endless hairpin curves
of that convict-built road, lunched at Nepenthe's, bought a
glimpse of the money wonders of San Simeon, and proudly
drove half-empty cars past stranded hitchhikers. The day over,
sights seen, they left the Sur, post cards in hand.

Not all those who profaned the Sur were transients.
Through each season there was Esalen, midway down the Sur,
third fork of a spiritual triangle the other two intersections of
which were P. T. Barnum and the Maharishi. I made my en-

trance to Esalen on the back of a pickup truck, having thrown my cycle over a cliff after it broke down for what I determined would be the last time. Standing by the road, thumb out, I was given a ride by a pseudo old-timer, a grey-bearded would-be patriarch, whose immediate judgment it was that I didn't know much about myself. That was for openers.

Though Esalen, dedicated to the exploration of human potential, was just then in a state of seige, resisting outsiders with a guard named Robot, the prophet wanted to show me a thing or two, and brought me in past the checkpoint. We walked down to a bathhouse that hung on a cliff over the ocean, and I sat back to watch him massage a young woman. As I watched him knead her skillfully, opening her ever so carefully, I began to feel that he did have something to teach me, and was just preparing to tell him so when he stopped, shook her leg, and said, "Is it good?"

I made my way out, strolled around the grounds, and made peace with Robot, purportedly a black belt in karate, a hustler who always got what he wanted, though he had no *Weltanschauung* to explain why or what or how. He knew only that the Esalen staff had some kind of hustle going, that they seemed oblivious to his games, and that they deferred to him. He was content.

I often returned to the baths after that initial visit, played a little music for the guests, and joined those middle-class professionals who were attracted to the idea of nude bathing in the sulfur baths (coed only at night), those hoping for a little promiscuity in a spiritually and intellectually earnest climate. Tinged with Bohemianism, an aura of hipness provided by the freaks who did the menial work, Esalen was a fine place for the liberal achiever who fancied himself a free thinker. There he could seriously shed those old confining values, shop through a catalogue of heresies, and purchase a new metaphysic. There too he could get freer with people, learn to touch them—let his pants down.

One night, sitting in the baths with a group of psychologists who were busy discussing the nature of human nature and the meaning of meaning, I was shaken out of my pipe dreams by Robot's order that everyone leave. It was a simple message: Get out or I'll wipe you out. Needless to say, discussions about the transparent self ceased pronto, and everyone rushed to save his skin.

Notwithstanding the drama of this particular class of his, Robot was not considered one of the staff. Though he was absolutely straight in his deviousness, Esalen had trouble learning from him. Pretensions obscuring its collective vision, Esalen thought that Zen was more formal stuff, and sought a better-pedigreed detergent for its psychomat.

In spite of the shills and hucksters, Robot aside, it was hard to argue with the baths, and I often returned to case into a tub, to look at the moon resting on the waves, and float through the night into the dawn. On one of my visits I was reminded that a hermit lived nearby, that his nephew had suggested that I look him up. Though advised by the Esalen staff that he was a wise man who cherished and enforced his solitude, I headed up to see him.

I arrived at his place, a beautiful home set on a cliff, and saw him out on the lawn, pacing up and down, hands behind his back, muttering to himself. He finally looked up, acknowledged my presence, and said that he had the answer. Trying to help, I asked him what the question was. Ah, the emperor's new clothes. What the hermit had discovered was that there were no clothes, that everyone lied, that the king was naked. I told him that I thought he was on the right track, presented my credentials, and was invited to stay.

I spent several days with him, and he seemed to appreciate the company. He was a terribly lonely man, so confused by the intricacies of human communication that he troubled himself trying to figure out what people were really saying. Conversations with him were always subject to instant replay, since he often stopped me in mid-sentence to ask what I had really meant by something I had said minutes before. In spite of this static on the lines, I liked him, and since I had no particular ax to grind, we got along. He seemed sad to see me go.

On my return to Esalen, after telling the staff that they had a lonely man up there on the cliff, I bumped into a freak who told me of a canyon on the Sur where people could stay without trouble. Tired of Esalen, disturbed by the physical development of the land, tired of the verbiage and the use of the property as a recommendation for the aesthetic caliber of its possessors, having to cope with the fact that the Sur was almost entirely private property, I decided to follow his lead.

I drove on down the coast highway, passing the few stores and their antihippy posters, and finally saw my place, a gate across from a small auto-graveyard. There, in that canyon, I met some refugees who had a vital relation to the Sur, who saw its blinking lights and flying saucers, who sought its shelter, who opened themselves to the immensity and power of the place. They understood perfectly that Big Sur was no person's property, but was rather a haven for those in need. It was more than a range of canyons and cliffs—each mountain was a giant sleeping with his head to the sea. Treated with respect, the giants would tolerate human presence, and would guide and protect those in need. Baked by the sun, chilled by the rains, those in the canyon stayed through the seasons, open to the wildness and serenity of the Sur, safe from the chaos and confusion of the world below.

· 13 ·
Billy

*And didn't he ramble on, in and out of town, till the
butchers cut him down, well didn't he ramble on. . . .*

Part One:
Billy on the Sur

When I first came up the mountain, pausing often under a fero-
cious sun, I passed a sentinel preoccupied with his meditation
and made my way up to a cluster of shacks which were
perched on, wedged between, and overshadowed by bould-
ers. It turned out that the population of this encampment
was comprised of ex-soldiers, ex-mental patients, ex-cons, and
flower children, all of whom had labored up the road, built
some shelter, and stayed.

Though I was appraised rather than welcomed, I finally

struck up a conversation with a man who introduced himself as Billy the Shoemaker, who was just then chomping down three tabs of acid, sitting at a bench smoking a joint, busy making sandals. He was a short, thin, forked radish of a man, with dark hair and a magnificent Zapata mustache ("a brush," he called it), a man who looked as though he had swum the Rio Grande on his way north, someone who might have been too tough for Sicily.

He had striking eyes, bright out of the darkness of his face, that did nothing to lessen the apprehension that he was both armed and dangerous. This intimidating appearance, however, was belied by his smile and missing front tooth, and the almost hostile reserve quickly gave way to humor and warmth. I learned that he was the politician of the place, the unsalaried mayor and curator of this remote looney bin, that he spent his time making hurt feelings better (he described his work as squaring and squashing beefs). He liked to guide the lives up there, and saw himself as guardian of the fragile stasis of the community. It suited him well, I came to see, to purposively pass his time bullshitting. He would sit there getting high, never as high as he wanted, exchanging gossip, telling stories of the last great episode in the life of the mountain. When forced he would work, but life in fact revolved around planning rather than implementation. Something big was always just around the corner.

In the course of meeting the residents of the mountain, listening to the endless cycles of stories, I learned that Billy had made his debut by walking up the road carrying a shotgun. By another path, moving toward him, came a man who looked like Valentino's double, wearing a white shirt and red cravat, sporting a pencil-like mustache, carrying an ax. They walked side by side up the mountain, each appraising the other from the corner of his eye, each waiting until Billy's opponent grudgingly admitted the presence of superior firepower, the shotgun and implacable impassivity, and introduced himself.

"I'm Mad Marcus of Venice, now of Big Sur," he said. Tasting the respect due from Billy replied, "I'm Billy the Shoemaker." That settled, Marcus allowed as how he had a little heroin, Billy produced an outfit, and they sat down to fix.

When I arrived Marcus was still in residence on the mountain, and was still, true to form, forever testing boundaries. As Billy once responded to my unspoken question, Marcus must have discovered that most people will do almost anything to avoid strife, and had turned that understanding into a way of life. The first time I met Marcus he was seated in a circle of people sharing some weed. When the joint reached him he toked not once but twice, reduced it nearly to roachlike proportions, smiled at the others, looked back at what was left of the joint with mellow appreciation, got up, and walked away with it. Needless to say, he broke all protocol in doing this, and left everyone stunned with his *chutzpah*.

If in that case he carried it off, standing twenty feet away grinning like the Cheshire cat, it was too much when he pilfered the pocketbook of the owner of the land while she was busy distributing free food to the settlement. In this instance, since she envisioned an art commune springing out of the arid soil, since no one wanted to disabuse her, a posse was formed, Marcus tracked down, and the money recovered.

Another time, at a gathering to celebrate the birth of a child, Marcus waited until the Big Sur drummers provided him with some cover and made off with a car, driving it to Monterey for a dope run. He came back several hours later, grinning from ear to ear, prepared if necessary to make some amends to the owners. Dope dealers that they were, however, they had no enthusiasm for the fact that he had taken their car, especially since it carried twenty kilos of super weed in the trunk. They beat him nearly to death.

As I stayed on, I learned that Marcus was in the habit of rising before anyone else in order to forage through the cars of visitors to the mountain, not taking everything, by no means, but shopping discriminately for just what he needed. I once rose at his hour, watched him, and strolled by while he was in the middle of his work. Startled, he looked at me for a moment, made his decision, and continued as before. My complicity in his work led me to be entitled to play cards with him. Marcus had a problem about losing, however, which strongly influenced his game. Whenever he saw a good hand coming on, he would raise me again and again, smiling right past whatever limit had been set, if for no other reason than to see what I'd do. I gathered that it was part of his theory of continuing education to try constantly to occupy that area of social space that was generally honored as no man's land.

Each afternoon he groomed carefully, somehow finding yet another starched and ironed white shirt, preening himself before a broken mirror, wearing nothing but that white shirt, waiting for the women on the mountain to be drawn to his dangling magnificence. Finally he would dress, walk around, and survey the day's crop of guests, quick to prey on easy game. More than once he disappeared off the mountain with a bevy of young girls, took their money, smoked their dope, played with them until he was bored, and then borrowed their car so that he could make it back to the Sur.

Though Marcus was a notorious figure on the Sur, though he measured up to and surpassed a reputation that reached even to the Haight-Ashbury ("Beware of Mad Marcus of Venice"), he was by no means the only person of stature in the mountain community. There was also Zebe, a large man who might have been a buccaneer in another life, a man whose present reincarnation was as gardener of that botanically inhospitable looney bin. And there should be no mistake that this was indeed a looney bin, a funny farm, that the names of its inhabitants, inscribed in the history of the Sur, were a roll call of the walking wounded, the shell-shocked of the war of twentieth-century life.

But it was Zebe who wore farmer's overalls without under-wear, those what must have been abrasive work pants, stomping around in his heavy boots, snorting with disdain at the arid soil, eking out the life of several huge sunflowers. Residents sympathetic to the difficulties of his work proposed to run hot-water pipes under the entire mountain and turn it into a tropical rain forest. This grand scheme, like so many others, was actually started. But no one, least of all Zebe (who worked harder than anyone else for those four long hours), expected to see the task finished. That was not the point.

Zebe carried a pair of hand shears on a thong at his side like a Burbankian Billy the Kid, and almost gratuitously trimmed random shrubs on the mountain. I once asked Billy what in God's name Zebe was doing. Billy looked at me, decided that it might possibly be worth trying to straighten me out, and said, "Well, maybe he likes to keep order." Zebe, meanwhile, had taken note of my reaction to his work, and the situation crystallized in a quick trip we made off the mountain to get some food. We drove down the coast, reached the store, and just as we headed inside Zebe stopped, took out his shears, and pruned a bush.

Back up on the mountain, ever willing to help the slow of mind, deciding that there must be something good in me some-where, Zebe took my problem as his own. One day in the blazing sun, long before the relief of the fog rolled up from the ocean, he guided me to the edge of the nearest promon-tory. Surveying the valley below, encompassing it with his eyes as if it were his private demense, he said, "You know, there's enough work here to keep a man busy for life."

Though there was in fact much to do, the residents of the mountain were careful to regulate the type of work in which they invested. They usually preferred the steadiness of routine, the familiarity of established procedures, and in any case, shied away from any task that threatened to remind them of the world below. One day, arguing with Billy about Billy's dilapidated stove, Zebe walked over and kicked it apart. Trying to catch up to Zebe's mood, Billy turned and busted his only window, only to have Zebe cuss him out for his stupidity, saying, "If that's the kind of fool you're going to be, we'll get the garden too." Zebe then walked over to the sunflower, pulled it out, and threw it at Billy. Several minutes later they were busy patching up the stove, papering over the window, replanting the flower. They then sat back to smoke a joint, sure that they had done a good day's work, glad they were never unemployed.

Some weeks later Zebe decided that a man with his responsibilities needed some stability, announced that it was time for a wedding, and chose in marriage the woman with whom he lived, a wraith who could be seen walking around the mountain in a long black dress, never known to have uttered a single word. On the appointed day Zebe came walking out of his shack buck-naked, top hat on his head, twirling a walking stick. Climbing to a boulder that overlooked the camp, met there by his bride (who was also naked except for the bracelets which ringed her arms), he waited with her until the sun just touched the rim of the horizon, and then, as old Pat whispered some words of wisdom, they copulated to the beating of many drums and the cheers of friends below.

Old Pat, who presided over the ceremony, was seen by Zebe as some kind of Zen master. A more realistic view was offered by Billy, who acknowledged that Pat was childlike, but knew also that he was "not quite right upstairs." Pat generally walked around the community in a towel and Hawaiian shirt, straw hat on his head, a man of perhaps fifty. He was much scarred by his exposure to life, particularly weathered by winters spent in a mud hogan, where he waited to see how long it would take for the rain to wash his shelter away, sharing the misery with his aged mother. Pat did, however, have a fine sense of theater, and when he thought it appropriate, would put on a brace of pistols and walk down to the road, there to take pot shots at passing tourists. He figured that that would give them something to write home about.

It was rumored that Pat's family had once owned the mountain, and he seemed to take this claim seriously, forever making plans for the improvement of the settlement, forever trying to regulate the lives of its residents. It was Pat, for instance, who was the original author of the rain-forest idea, and it was also Pat who called a town meeting (a council fire) to announce his plan to bring electricity to the mountain, to install street lamps and incorporate the place as a city.

His more important work, however, was as a social worker. Not without method in his madness, Pat struggled like Noah to gather things in pairs, to match everything up, two by two. With this kind of a mandate, he was much troubled by a woman who lived alone in one of the shacks. Even Billy conceded that this situation might cause strife, particularly if she were not monogamous. Quick to spot her vice, that she liked sex but not men, Pat paraded back and forth before her hut, naked with penis erect, until she left.

It was also part of Pat's master plan to get rid of Billy, primarily because he felt that Billy threatened his position as king of the mountain. Accordingly, he arrived at Billy's shack one morning spruced up in a coat and tie, invited Billy's wife up to pay him a visit, gave her a big wink, patted her on the ass, and headed off. No fool, Pat had taken note of difficulties in the marriage, and figured that he had a way to get at Billy. He was still waiting at his hut, back to the window, when Billy reached in, put a skinning knife to his throat, and uttered these immortal words: "You know Pat, I don't much like you anyway, and if you were dead I wouldn't have to see you no more."

A feud of sorts went on between them for a while, until Billy learned that Pat was trying to get a gun. He walked up to Pat's place, rifle in hand, and gave it to him, saying, "You know, no one will give you a gun because they think you're crazy, but I know why you want it, so here." That gesture ended the feud. It was delicate business, to be sure, but they both understood that some balance had to be maintained.

Billy himself never wavered in his belief that these were beautiful people, crazy (he used the word "ringy") perhaps, but beautiful. More than once he spoke of his feeling that there was no place in the world below for people who could not bend. Some people just couldn't make the accommodations. They needed shelter, and received it from the Sur. Grateful in their fashion, though they often went wild, the members of the community exercised just enough restraint to prevent violence, just enough control to keep from giving the zealous Monterey police cause to invade their sanctuary. It took much diplomacy, but they had all the time in the world.

Even Marcus, mad as he was, received care after he was injured in an accident. Even he understood that it was a community, though bizarre, that it protected its own. As Billy was quick to point out, Marcus never really bothered any of the Sur people. Nor was Marcus incorrect when he assumed that those who lived in the camp would make allowances for his particular form of self-defense.

The camp was also united in its view of the various two-bit hustlers who made their way up the mountain to try their hand against the masters. One of these, Brother Joseph, appeared one day in yachting whites and a commodore's hat, only to exchange that costume for a long staff and robe. Also known as Joe the Hustler, Brother Joseph was always first in line for dope and cigarettes, coming on with that I-am-the-Church-so-feed-me look whenever he thought he could carry it off. The regulars were disgusted by such a bad routine. When he first arrived, before he saw the light, Joe had tried to outfox Marcus, but wound up losing a car, two credit cards, and his dope stash. Stunned, he decided to stay for some lessons.

He was accompanied by a huge girl with scabby legs who made a nightly performance of her showers. Standing in the clearing, drafting two or three hippies into the work of holding a sheet to screen her nakedness, she insisted that everyone honor a lady's modesty and avert their eyes. Taking this all in, looking at the hippies holding her cover, Billy winced and said that they were providing a public service and didn't know it.

In time Brother Joseph developed a brogue, donned his sea clothes once more, and came out of the mountains with a girl he presented as his bride. It was rumored that she had a lot of money, and even Billy grudgingly conceded that Joe had learned a thing or two. Not long after Joseph took his leave, speaking of plans for a new life in Florida, accompanied by his wife and a troupe of innocents. Pat muttered something about feed them to the alligators, and they were gone.

Each night, cold and stoned, just under the stars, the residents of the mountain would give voice to their art. All visitors and inhabitants of the Sur were willy-nilly characters in a great and unending work of oral literature, an ongoing and ever-richer epic. This form generally commenced with a simple rhetorical question, such as, "Do you remember that crazy motherfucker so and so?" or, "Do you remember when that crazy motherfucker did such and such?" The memory of a man once evoked, his shade, gave rise to stories, anecdotes, parables, fables, encomia, eulogies, and panegyrics. It was at these times that Billy, working on his leather, smoking a joint, passing a bottle of wine, played both Homer and Aesop, breathing life into memories, making his points, telling his tales.

In these terms Billy savored the memory of Trader Jim, now in the pantheon of the immortals, who came up the mountain one day to do some trading, dressed as usual in buckskins, stash pouches swinging from his belt. It was Jim's vision of the frontier way that one always sat down to trade as a preliminary to socializing. Since he never had much to say, it was in fact his *raison d'être*. Though not in his particular movie, the Sur people tolerated his style. It was part of the code, though Jim was an inveterate bullshitter, a man forever compelled to leave himself with the shitty end of the stick. He was, as Billy said, a redneck.

In any case, Jim came up that day, immolated in his buckskins, still smarting from the recent decline of his tribe of redskins, a troupe of teeny boppers from Los Angeles who for a time had been his followers. Apparently he had done quite well until he said to one of the boys, "Hey brave, fetch me some food." Somehow that line pushed just too far, and Jim lost both braves and squaws. Nevertheless, though he knew that his defeat was already part of the literature, he managed a smile, his buzzard head bobbing out of control on that red neck, gizzard working, and said "Howdy, brother." This was always offensive to Billy, for by no stretch of the imagination could he see Jim as his brother. Respecting protocol as he did, diplomat that he was, he was sure that Jim knew better. But in his fine noncommittal way, ever tactful, Billy returned the greeting.

Jim sat down in the shade and unhooked his trading pouch. It was a leather bag embossed with a number eight, to whit, a golf-club cover, and from it he pulled rosary beads, a penknife, four marbles, an elastic band, several hash pipes, and a dark brown lump. Taking in the merchandise, letting a few moments pass, Billy asked what the lump was. "Opium," Jim said. Calmly, Billy asked to see it. He took the lump in his hand, worked it under his thumb, rolled it around, smelled it, tossed it in the air and then, in one fast and totally devastating (to Jim) move, popped the entire piece in his mouth and swallowed it. Disbelieving, Jim strained to find the right words. But Billy spoke first. "Yup, brother, that sure was opium." He smiled, picked himself up, and walked away.

Each night the litany of stories carried the camp into morning, and the cycle rolled onward without landmarks in time, high above the sunsets, far above the ocean. Late each afternoon there was always a little time for the endless gathering of materials for works forever in progress, desperation inhering only in the quest for cigarettes and dope.

Occasionally, in and around the stories, the quarrels, and the vendettas, given the force of the mountain, the weight of the sky, and the clouts of the sun—all this and a little too much dope—occasionally one would hear talk of flying saucers, and perhaps see them himself. Stoned one night, down at the beach, Billy witnessed the landing of Martian ambassadors to Big Sur. Rushing back up the mountain, he shot some heroin to get his head straight, it being his conviction that while high on heroin he was cold, clear, impartial, and objective. One could tell him no lies, no alibis. Picking up his rifle he headed back to the site, waiting long hours in the darkness, and finally returned to report that the coast was clear, that there were no longer any aliens in the neighborhood. Big Sur had survived again.

Somewhere along the line, though just when it would be impossible to precise, I found myself far up on a cliff over the beach, teeth chattering, wondering first how I got there and second how I was to get down. Pulling myself together, I was transformed into Sir Edmund Hillary, a human fly, suction cups on each finger and toe, and descended with the surety of a Sherpa tribesman. On solid ground, thinking it over, I had the feeling that things were getting out of hand. I was confirmed in this sensation on my return to camp by a message penciled by old Pat on the wall of Billy's shack. It read: "The mountain lion said to the racoon, 'Let's go down to the gymnasium and listen to the sweat'."

Feeling suddenly that it was now or never for me to leave, I rushed down the mountain, got into my bus, and headed north up the coast highway toward Berkeley. I felt the engine working and eased back with relief. But as I neared the edge of the Sur a cacophony of voices screamed out to me, as the mountains, the trees, the moon, the stars, the sleeping giants, the ghosts, and all the human lives of the Sur, both past and present, called out for me to stay, shrieking that I was now part of the Sur, warning me, pleading with me, telling me that I was leaving my refuge behind. Fool that I was I pressed on, and the voices faded slowly, though they continued to ring in my ears. They were right, of course, since as I moved further and further from the mountain there was only Esalen, Nepenthe's, Carmel, and Oakland.

Part Two:
Billy off the Sur

"What's so good about good-bye?"

Several months later, back in Berkeley, I was surprised to find Billy, his wife, and their son on my doorstep. Though I had assumed that Billy was capable of choosing to live in a place other than Big Sur, though I knew something of his history and ambitions, I located him so precisely on that mountain top that I was startled to see him anywhere else.

For the next year and more we saw much of each other, sharing mutual dreams and jokes, both indulging in visions of our future success and appreciating our ineptness. We became, over time, partners, complemented each other, and knew it. If we understood too that his young wife was correct when she said that time had slowed Billy down, whatever he might once have been, he was in that period my mentor, minister of protocol, guide, side-kick, friend, and companion in an endless performance of Don Quixote in which we constantly traded and fused the roles of knight and squire, or each played both simultaneously. The duration of our friendship was a time of learning for me, of teaching for him. We each sought and enjoyed the work.

Our friendship ended with his death. Yet that only made

something abstract quite final. We had both been remiss. I learned of his death by phone, and found confirmation of what I would not believe in the local newspapers. Recording his death as a murder, they described the victim as a known narcotics user. In addition they relayed the information that the deceased was a former felon who had served time in both the Los Angeles County Jail (nine months) and in San Quentin (four years), who was at the time of his death charged with attempted murder. He had, they wrote, accused a neighbor of consorting with his wife and then shot him in the ear. Though the papers failed to report it, the trial for this alleged offense was imminent. Nor did the papers point out that as an ex-felon he was almost sure to be found guilty. The only question was how much time he would do, or, as he decided, how much time he could do.

The information presented by the newspapers was more or less accurate. None of it, of course, spoke for his life. Outlines were drawn, yet there is no one of us who would not balk at so spare a résumé of his being, no one of us who could abide standing so naked, so classified, so bereft of the substance which composed his life one day and the next. At the very least, in keeping with the tone of the newspaper stories, it should be pointed out that Billy was terrified of the prospect of a return to prison, that he was very desperate, and even dangerous. There was no escape for him and he ran madly. He was trapped and squealing, and, in a roundabout way, found someone to put him out of his misery. In ripping off a heroin dealer, he knew that either he would be shot or that the heroin would simply ease the pain until he died another way, at another rate. He had given up.

I went down to the morgue with his wife, driving past a sign advertising the comforts of cold storage, and entered an office lined with awards commending the paucity of employee accidents. Near the door a sign admonished visitors to mind the stairs. Death was well ordered, even if life was chaotic, and it was with a civil servant that we went to see him. There he lay, behind a glass door, coiffed in a sheet like a pharaoh. His wife signed the appropriate forms, claimed him as her own, and we left.

The Veterans Administration and the Social Security Office provided funds for the funeral of an ex-GI on welfare, so we had a gathering. His friends and acquaintances (hippies, junkies, street people, and some others, though no blood kin) came together to talk and to say good-bye. The anthem was by The Band: "Music from Big Pink." They had the message: "Tears of rage, tears of grief—I shall be released." Not only did the words feel right, but he had more than once sat in my house singing that song. It seemed a good way to say goodbye. I lifted the lid of the coffin, took a last look at him, and parted, searching for his boy.

His legacy to this world was a wife and two young sons, some debts, and, because he was a veteran, an American flag. Yet he himself, immortal to the degree that he lives in the memories of those who survived him, is still very much present, and though I miss him, or, rather, because I even now expect to see him at any moment, I find it hard to mourn. Beyond this, he was too tired to begrudge him some rest. He had faced more prison, further blows to his manhood. He did not believe that he could pass any more of that kind of time.

Those at the funeral, many seeing a dead man for the first time, some just then viewing the paradigm of their own worst impulses, came together intentionally, explicitly, because he died. Yet his death induced few changes. What was the moral? Give up drugs? Get a job? Leave Berkeley? Billy seemed an exception since all present knew that he had gone wild, destroying himself too blatantly, imperiling others too directly.

That was really the point. His death had no sting because he had broken the rules. The junkies present were not about to kick because he was dead. Rather, his death was a good reason to fix—commiseration. And no one else seemed to get any closer to life through his death. Since he had gone too far, become too direct in his confrontation with not-life, the guests at his funeral chose to relate to his life rather than to the meaning of his death. If in life he was exceptional, to the degree that his death was also seen as exceptional no one profited from it.

When alive, he had been one man's friend, another's enemy, a good man, a weak man, a junkie, a leather worker, an ex-con, a side-kick—whatever. In death he was not so easily confronted. His body, lifeless, spoke too heavily for that part of us all that was death-in-life, so we turned our thoughts and feelings to what he had been before, when he lived, and spoke in life for our lives, not in death for our deaths.

At his best he was a man who loved his family and friends, who cared deeply about his craft and worked it well. At his worst he was full of self-pity and self-contempt, unreliable, directionless, a whipped cur. I came to love him, to learn respect for a man whose form of self-respect was often defiance. Like the fox in Saint-Exupéry's *The Little Prince* he taught me how to tame him. He used to tell me not to put him under a microscope. Though it proved hard and sometimes incorrect to presume no inalterable distance between us, I tried to get past unearned categories, set up a few rules of my own, and there we were. Though he often doubted his own motives, though I was often ingenuous, we were in fact close friends. It was part of his hell that he could not trust himself, part of mine that I did not help him more.

In the end he was without hope. His mother, he once told me, had drunk a lot of wine and had tricked to earn some money. His father died young, bitter and worn out. Part Indian, Billy sometimes saw himself as a nigger, in the worst sense of the word. While in San Quentin he was called Crazy Nick. On Big Sur he was Billy the Shoemaker. For me he was and is simply Billy. I can see him now, in my mind's eye, in candids, Billy tinkering with the car, Billy on the run, Billy walking with his boy, Billy working leather. He could dream, he never did kick his habit, and a part of him wanted to die. His life was in fact as small as any, but his visions were grand, he had integrity, and he had the poise of a man who knew himself well. Though constantly in need, he seldom imposed.

Everyone takes from death, as from life, what they want. One of Billy's friends, a sergeant without an army, sunk deeper into his misery after Billy died. Others forgot, slipping past Death the Cop as though they were holding. What I retain most is the tone of the days we shared, the strength of a bond one trusted and enjoyed, the honestness of the man within the framework of his faults.

He came off the Sur because he felt that he was getting crazy up there. Though he dealt successfully with the lost people of the mountain, he perceived correctly that he played their games well, and more, helped define them. Dealing in terms they could understand, he reached the point where he could barely establish distance between himself and the general flow of madness. Living so remote from the larger culture, he imagined that there was something for him in the world below.

He should have known better. In the thirty-three years of his life he had never had an easy time. He stayed on the Sur because he was tired of maintaining a posture of continual defensive offense. Fighting on the block as a child and young man, hassling in the service, doing time, he had been beaten down, become more devious, and had lost his resilience. He kept learning, but concluded that the lessons were too costly, that they were killing him. Notwithstanding the protection of the Sur, however, he did not feel that he could sustain a life there. He had a wife and child to care for: he thought he wanted something more stable, an environment in which he could live by using his skills as a craftsman. Or perhaps this construct of his thoughts imputes too much intentionality to his actions. Perhaps he simply drifted to the Sur, drifted off it, and was unable to return.

Billy was raised in Detroit, where he lived in an area in which it was accepted that if someone came home with a thousand dollars no one asked where it came from. One just stuck out his hand. As Billy described the street scene in which he grew up, people have vices, and some people live on them.

He left Detroit to enter the service, outlasted a redneck sergeant ("he told me when to shit and what color"), and was sent over to Okinawa. There, seeing another culture, smoking a lot of dope, tuning into Buddhism, he first tasted the idea that there might be something beyond the street life in which he had been raised. There too he began to read, initially because he felt ignorant (there were a number of college draftees in his unit), and then because he was spellbound by the worlds books opened up to him, mesmerized by stories of lives so unlike his own.

During his time in the service he also found reinforcement for his dislike of those in power: He was forever doing extra push-ups with a full pack on his back for failing to follow orders; he fought it out with a corporal who was pushing him too hard; and he had no use for the officers who seemed so aloof, who eased their pains in their comfortable clubs.

His time was finally up, and he came out to Los Angeles, living on his severance pay, running with friends from the service, reading books. In time, however, he found his partners settling down, and he began to look for something to do, for some money. He dealt dope for six months, took a fall, went to jail, got out, dealt for a year and a half, was set up by his cousin, and went back to prison, this time for four years.

The four years was a long time. He seldom spoke much about that period, feeling that most of the people he knew had been inside, and that those who hadn't could never relate to it, or would be interested only in atrocities, not in the routine and the sheer killing passage of time. Occasionally, however, wanting to explain something to me, he would speak about

San Quentin. He told me once that he had no visitors for the entire length of his term, though one day his number had been called and he ran toward the rotunda, breaking the rules by moving so fast, getting there only to be informed by one of the oakie guards that there had been a mistake.

He was considered crazy by the inmates because he would not subscribe to the kind of narcissism that most men observed, keeping clothes perfectly ironed, shoes shined, constantly grooming and preening, loving themselves and therefore, presumably, being worthy of being loved by others. Billy would have none of it, and was therefore considered crazy, deemed all the more insane because he allowed no intrusion of his air space, because he insisted, violently, on his privacy.

Talking about the flow of time inside, Billy told me that he usually ate a pint of ice cream each night, a sensual luxury, that he would sit alone making plans not to escape but to wipe out all the guards and prisoners, the sea gulls too, in order to have some silence. And he would read, and think, trying not to drift into depression, but often wanting to die, to stop the erosion of his youth.

While in San Quentin he met a teacher who valued his life, who gave him the opportunity to lower his guard, and Billy melted before so gentle, so nakedly honest a man. As he phrased it, he met himself for the first time, and confronted his terrible loneliness, the lack of love in his world. Though he had always known how to seem sincere, he told me, to use sincerity as a ploy, he admitted the lie to himself while in prison, and searched for truths. He meditated.

When he first met the teacher, who came into the prison several nights a week, Billy didn't know what to make of the man. He told himself that the guy was a punk, but kept going back to see him, and began to speak with him, talking about soil, plants, anything that was alive, and would sometimes tell him something about himself. Learning trust, Billy would go back to the yard to listen to men tell stories, just listening, giving them the comfort of running their pains and dreams out to him, learning to admit his own humanity. He said that in the teacher he met an honest man, and became his pupil.

In prison too, however, he learned to be con-wise. He kept his distance, never spoke with a hack, and became adept at pinpointing another man's strengths and weaknesses, skillful enough to run games to provide himself with whatever he wanted, to maintain enough affability or craziness to be left alone. He learned to read all the types of affiliations that defined turf; he learned protocol. But above all he learned that he was a loser. One could have style, class, be straight, fight the man, put him on, game him, humor him, or obey him, but the man was the man, a prisoner a prisoner.

Coming out of San Quentin, having seen so many forms of death and murder, he went to work in a shoe-repair shop and hustled chess in Berkeley bars at night, drawing on the expertise of four years of steady practice. Not all the time inside had been wasted.

On the street, however, things weren't as well structured as in prison. He had learned too well to define himself in opposition to the guards, the system, to rest his strength on the foundation of constant battle. In Berkeley he found a home, married, and had a son. He worked steadily and found some stability. Yet he could not give up his use of heroin, his self-pity, nor could he relinquish a stance in which he had invested so much time and pain. He was always sure that he could spot a junkie, and himself be spotted. He saw himself as a walking misdemeanor, and could not conceive of a different role. In a profound sense he had become institutionalized. Hard as he had fought, he believed their definition of him, was overwhelmed by their power, and carried the prison with him when he walked out the gate. Though he had some chances, he could not take them.

It was at the point that he found himself buying a three-hundred-dollar bedroom set that he decided to head for the

Sur. From the time he decided to cut loose, having been straight for about as long as he could, he never again gained enough stability to have any hope of a life with some continuity. From that day on, seeing only lower bourgeois life as an alternative, he committed himself to hustling. He made the mistake of oversimplifying the choices, and was doomed.

When he came off the Sur he landed in the ghetto of Berkeley, blacks, winos, and hippies for neighbors, committing himself to hassles with minor bureaucrats, landlords, and the police. Though he was substantially correct in his contempt for their contempt of him, though he was straighter and more honest than they would ever be, he condemned himself to being at their mercy. He was right, of course, when he caught his slumlord trying to turn off the water and threw him against the wall, but he was evicted anyway. And with all the battles, with the constant struggle to get enough momentum and money to put it together, he never brought anything to completion, forever gathering equipment and materials, too far below any economy of scale to make anything from his work.

So he settled for being right, for the associations with men who, though slipping themselves, were also strong in their honesty, in their understanding of the bullshit that geared most people's lives, in their respect for losers of quality. And though there was always the promise of getting past the margin, though we more than once went through the ceremony of breaking his outfits, he was slowly worn down, turning back to heroin to get a rest, falling asleep in the leather chair in his living room, leather scattered over the sewing machines, half-finished vests and skirts on the table, three or four semipermanent and destitute visitors in the bedroom.

In Berkeley, marveling at the freeness of the hippies, watching them lose their youth too quickly, he thrived in so uncombative a world, yet he was always too close to the edge. To work in leather, the way he said he wanted, required both a tranquility he did not have and capital he would never gain.

And in a sense he wanted neither. For to have all the requisites might have demanded performance he was not sure he could execute. And to be too stable would destroy, he thought, his relationship to the men he counted as his friends because they, like himself, were beyond the pale. Once one became too instrumental vis à vis his environment, Billy thought, he came to use people. Billy preferred not to risk that possibility.

Surrounded by friends, always busy, he nevertheless had a keen sense of the lostness of the lives around him. Once, as I reacted with dismay to the news that one of his wife's husbandless friends was pregnant once again, he said quietly that the girl didn't think that she could ever have the man she wanted, and so asked for the child. He was right, of course, but one had to have lost a great many illusions to be able to accept this as the best one could do.

In the early months of our friendship he seldom introduced me to his friends, sure that I would violate the protocol and in so doing reveal my feeling of superiority to them. It was a long and slow lesson he wanted to teach me, to have me learn compassion. His dignity and tact, his distinction between victims and executioners, allowed for no unwarranted rudeness or contempt. Over time, feeling that I had learned respect, he brought me around, each friend a doper or ex-con, each one slow to speak, waiting until it was clear that only friends were present. All generous with each other, none could offer more than human support, for in turn each fought to survive.

For a while Billy thought that he could make it, and got up each morning at five to work as a hot walker down at the race track, exercising the horses, getting into shape himself. It was the kind of job he liked, work that put him inside the action, not minding at all that he didn't own the horse, content to know that he was really the one who made things happen. Typically, however, his ideas conflicted with his superior's, and he was fired.

Money in his pocket, he began to work in leather again,

making everyone just what they wanted, unable to bring himself to charge enough to pay even for his materials. But he enjoyed the work, and it left him plenty of time to be with his boy. Sometimes, drifting through the afternoon, Billy would walk around town, hustling a little, just watching his son take in the universe. He loved to be around his son, and the boy, independent as he was, liked nothing more than to have Billy with him when he chased buses and ran after dogs.

From time to time Billy joined me in visits to my friends, but read in most of them a contempt for others that he could not abide, and found their politics pointless at best. He considered it a given that he would always be on the outside, no matter what the regime, and saw too little real compassion in my peers, a sense of rectitude and the arrogance of ignorance that would leave them as corruptible by power (and the lack of it) as those they condemned.

Playing chess with one of my friends, sipping wine between moves, he smiled with victory because he knew that his opponent had been certain of winning. After all, Billy was an ex-con and a doper. Though the smile was as far as he would push the lesson, Billy had no use for such presumption, and generally referred to such people as punks. He used the word not to say that they were homosexual, or even that they would be homosexual if in prison, but rather to say that as quick as they were to put themselves above others, they would be just as quick to crawl to save their skins. He never belabored the point. He simply made it clear that he chose his people carefully, and waited for me to do the same.

Out of work, he began to spend more time on the block again, selling a little weed, searching for materials, borrowing a car, lending someone in need a little money he did not have for himself, rapping with his friends. When it went well, hustling kept him busy and in rent money, providing plenty of opportunities for him to socialize with everyone he knew. Months could pass without notice. There were no blue Mondays and no holidays. Each day was the same, some more successful than others, but all devoted to earning just enough money to pay the rent, to dabbling in now one project and then another, making someone a vest, planning to fix someone's boat for him, putting an old car back together, drinking coffee on Telegraph Avenue, getting high.

Seasons changed, however, and soon he was too low on money, depressed, and ill. All the dope had taken its toll, and he nearly died. In the process of recovering, his love for his wife came into focus once again, and he was happy. One day, still weak, he heard someone enter his house, gathered that it was the same peeping Tom who had been bothering his wife, grabbed his gun, and fired. A moment later he was on the run, running for his life, trying to get past the police. For a while he hid with friends in Richmond, but finally turned himself in. He was too tired to go any further. As he once said of a friend who lost his wife, it was suicide but they didn't bury him. For though he could not leave, though he could not run with a wife and child, though he was too worn to run alone and unwilling to leave them behind, he could not go back to prison. He had reached a cul-de-sac.

It should have been obvious what he was going to do. Perhaps some of his friends knew, though they said nothing. I myself wanted to believe that he would somehow be freed, that he would have a chance to put his life together, to bring his competence to fruition. But peace was what he sought, and he was too much a man to accept the tranquility of living death inside the walls of a prison.

When he had first told me never to put him under a microscope, never to take the stance that I subsumed him, I understood that he had something to teach me, and accepted the friendship on those terms. In so many ways he was right, showing me in the most subtle ways that I made unwarranted distinctions between myself and others, that I presumed myself immune from the elemental forces which he had seen sweep through his life and the lives of those closest to him. Further, his moral sense derived its deepest compulsion from prison, where there were only hacks and inmates in the world, where there was no one in between. He made me vividly aware of the capacity of anyone with power, even the slightest edge, to treat those beneath him with contempt.

Beyond this, he used heroin. He was not a junkie, though he used the word, to the degree that he never committed a crime to support his habit, nor was his dependence on heroin steady or substantial. Heroin was simply something to which he could turn, and often did. Though he was forever swearing to kick once and for all, though he avoided me when he was using, he also felt that a heroin habit was no worse than the vices of most people, that a man was entitled to use it. What he never made explicit was that most junkies die young, and that as a vehicle for association, junk brought him in contact only with those who had lost hold on life. This is not to say that the occasional use of heroin doomed anyone. It is only to say that in fact very few people used heroin occasionally.

Throughout my friendship with him, he never lied, never wavered in his readiness to help me, and was more trustworthy than any man I knew. He made no boasts, and did precisely what he said he would do. Yet at the same time he misread the world. A man must learn some accommodation to power or condemn himself to a marginal life which will break him. Billy and his friends were men I trusted and respected for their tact and honesty, but they had given up, settling for style in the mode of death. They never saw another way.

Billy had long held a fantasy about the Orient, wanting to get further into Zen, dreaming of one day living in the East. The year in Okinawa and the teacher in San Quentin had moved him. Yet he was never able to find a middle ground between the world of hacks and inmates, between those who used and those who were used. It was enough for him to be sure that such a place, such a man, were so exceptional as to be functionally unreal. He could not afford to trust in them. The meek, he was sure, would never inherit the earth.

So he died tough. In love, several months earlier, I had given him a gold fob watch. It suited him well, such a well-crafted and sturdy timepiece, and he consulted it often though we both knew he had no schedule to keep. I can remember his reaction to the gift, a diffidence and surprise that life had given him something beautiful once again.

After his death I found that he had pawned the watch. It speaks to his life that he sold too cheaply what he valued most. Once, having spent the day with his son, wandering with that source of constant wonder and love, he sat with me rapping. I asked him where, in all the world, he wanted to be. "Right here, my friend," he said, "right here."

He once told me, speaking of his boy, that the child would die unless cared for. And somehow he himself never found the right care. He always lived on the margin, was forever searching for a way to put it together. He accomplished very little in concrete terms, yet he was never a man one measured by what he produced. His understanding and his humor, his quiet advocacy of the tired and the poor, his raps and his integrity were his art and his work, though he found no way to mold his being into a marketable commodity.

I did not see him the last months of his life. Perhaps the point was that he believed in me, that though I was to learn to understand (not to pity or condemn) the world he made his own, I was always to be beyond it, free, safe from what he knew to be life itself. Warning signs he disregarded, perhaps out of that secret desire to make me really understand his life, to experience it no holds barred, as he did. Yet within limits it was our differences he cherished. He did not want me to be like him. When it became clear that my lessons were to be firsthand, he cast me, as he had cast himself, from his heart. I

185

became too much like him. My pain was his. He reacted with despair, disappeared, and went off, alone, to bring his misery to an end.

His ashes are now strewn over the ocean, and his name is inscribed on the wall of the men's room in the Café Mediterraneum. He has left his mark. He would have appreciated the fact that I was prohibited by law, by lobby, from taking his remains to Big Sur. He would have nodded quietly, unblinking, at the procedures we had to follow to lay him to rest. Had he been there to comment on the hassles he might have said "sheeuut," or, counseling acceptance of the inevitable, he might have told me that there was no way to change such things, "no way atall."

My friend Billy, the motherless child, is gone, and leaves me bereaved. God gave him the rainbow sign, and the fires came. It's time for good-byes.

> oh, billy, your death has taken me by surprise
> the night comes fast
> the orphan is dying to see its mother

· 14 ·
Those
Billy
Left
Behind:
Danny

"For man must have his fling, and every dog his day."

In the period after Billy's death the elements closed in, and for weeks those who survived him pushed on through rain and cold. The optimism of a local astrologer notwithstanding, the only people proven correct just then were the indigenous Cassandras. During those months, too many bummers to share, the prospect of further bad times led me to indulge myself in the thought that I might have entered the world, in my present incarnation at least, at the wrong time, the wrong place, and in (with) the wrong manner(s). I harbored the suspicion that I had been too quick to make my way into the world, that perhaps I should have held out my finger to test the prevailing postwar wind, to have had some reading of what I was getting myself into.

In the face of recurrent and imminent bad times, having seen the fallacies of intentional action, I came to place such faith as I had in serendipity. That is to say, I took refuge in my apparent capacity to make desirable discoveries by accident. As a program, serendipity demanded little more than staying alive. Whatever one did, was.

Such a style, the use of which became ever more prevalent, marked the end of a confidence that took what then seemed a long time to undermine. Though a trust in serendipity eliminated the tragic (every stick has two handles; *que sera, sera*) it was also an admission of defeat. No longer was there claim to purposive and causal bravery, or, at least, bravery became inadvertent. Heroism, in the old mold, was for someone else, and everyone I knew was struggling to find his way in the darkness of daylight-savings time.

It was in this period that I ran into Danny, a man who had been one of Billy's closest friends, godfather to his child. We had first met when Billy was on the run, and I remembered Danny for counseling Billy to do his time only once, not to live it in his imagination. He calmed Billy, and made it clear that there was no alternative, that Billy would have to go back to prison. He addressed his energies to helping Billy face that fact, speaking for long hours with him, getting high with him, working with him through the fear, the loss, the sadness.

Danny was Irish, in his mid-thirties, face worn, eyes tired, hair laced with white. He was always quiet, even withdrawn, and seemed not so much shy as constantly shying away. Occasionally he would join a conversation, suddenly jumping in to tell a story, animated, strong, smiling, and one had a glimpse of his past. He was the kind of man who elicited trust and affection, who would have been the first to charge the enemy lines to rescue a wounded friend. But the wars were different now, and he fought to stay alive after five years in prison for possession of marijuana, and the loss of his wife to another man.

Though he never said so, it was apparent that he considered the world a wasteland.

He had often turned to heroin for solace, and was once again wedded to his habit, uninterested in sex, unable to defecate. Two rest cures, courtesy of the state, had propped him up, filled him out, and left him briefly with a small pot belly. Within the confines of his retreat he had done the work given him, and said that he enjoyed the responsibility. But now he was lean and wasted, worn down by racing between cheap Shattuck Avenue hotels and Telegraph Avenue, running a gauntlet of police, creditors, and those who simply didn't like or wouldn't help him. The attack, having started slowly (he had even found a job), was now in full force.

Taking strength in weakness he had cultivated a heavy habit, only to so exhaust the veins of his body that he had poisoned himself in the search for yet another opening, and was now in danger of losing his leg if he did not get help. Meanwhile, he had sheltered others more wretched than himself, recklessly, defiantly, and had stumbled quickly into three busts, any one of which was enough to put him back inside.

At the same time, trying to support his habit, he had taken heroin on credit to sell, but could not stomach refusing the stuff to those who could not pay, those who while doomed by the habit nevertheless suffered if they could not feed it. In his generosity (aware that it carried the wish for companionship in misery, aware that he had known he would not sell the heroin), he lost his business reputation on the street, a precious thing, and was being hounded to pay up.

All of this, however, he almost welcomed. Each flurry of trouble, much of which he incurred with some kind of intentionality, only brought him closer to the end. In prison, at least, he could get his leg cared for and be free from fear about unpaid debts. Sure that he knew how to do easy time, sure that he would not fight a confinement that had its benefits, aware that being on his own had come to be a killing interval between stretches of incarceration, he was not about to struggle.

He did not say directly, of course, that he welcomed prison. That kind of despair was unspeakable. Certain forms had to be maintained. Yet both of us understood that once the handle for putting things together was lost, it could be impossible to find. As Danny said, "I ain't doin' no good here."

We talked for a while, and both of us willingly turned the conversation to the time when it was his care and strength that carried Billy on. In that period I had great respect for his love and tact. Though beaten himself, knowing that he lived with friends most of whom would fail, Danny managed to dismiss paranoia and pessimism without getting dirty in the lie. As a junkie whose friends also had habits, he understood that they, like himself, could be together one day and strung out the next. He understood also that a man with a habit, knowing his own instability, could demand more than a fair share of trust, and then betray it.

Beyond this, he felt without excusing himself that a heroin habit was only an exaggeration of the weaknesses of all men. They, he felt, like himself, warranted a certain modicum of respect simply for being alive. And with his friends it was never failure alone that formed the bond. Rather, it was that, within the confines of a propensity to fail, each manifested unmistakable strength and compassion.

Our conversation soon ended. Since he was avoiding mutual friends, since he knew that I drew back from the death he carried, we had little left to say to each other. He moved to split, saying by his gestures that he could only bring me down, that he wished to save us both the hassle. Without self-pity, he was saying that he was a loser, that he didn't want to jinx me. Or, even, that some part of him might want to, but that he wouldn't.

As he moved to go he stopped and offered a line of poetry

("The flowers wince at the rude goodness of the rain, but they drink"). He did not claim the line as his own, fearing perhaps that I would not believe him. And he had, of course, far too much delicacy to make me confront the ugliness of my suspicions. So he walked away, waving with bravado, summoning a smile. He was trying to tell me, I think, that he might have the strength for one more comeback. But he knew too that I understood how tired a man could be.

When he had been born, he once told me, life had embraced him and said, "Okay, lover, make your first mistake." And that's how it had gone. He now saw no way to hustle himself out of his troubles. His kind of strength, his direct and physical courage, wasn't supple enough to extricate him from such a whirlpool. It was too late.

In this bleak period those friends of mine who best struggled against the downward pull weren't doing well. Billy, for one, was dead. Some whom I respected from afar tried to fight it out. But most, like Danny, seemed to have put their fortunes in the laps of the gods, still pretending, even, to be looking for one thing, but sure, beyond doubt, that they would find something very different.

· 15 ·
Those
Billy
Also
Left
Behind

"Say the word and you'll be free."

It was in this season too that the survivors of a social movement gathered to enjoy the largesse of a man who, through them, had made it. Yet what was to be a child of joy was for me a misshapen dwarf, a grotesque homunculus aping true sentiments, the product of a marriage between belated generosity and a lack of real compassion and memory.

In short, it was a success party, a testament to the fortitude of an entrepreneur and some of those who three long years before had been swept up in the commercial implications of Ken Kesey's acid visions. On the surface, nothing went wrong, but something bad, very bad, the worse for being ignored, kept trying to intrude.

The evening started with the music of a trio (harp, bass clar-

192

inet, and flute) to accompany dinner. It was a kind of parody (could it have been intentional?) of what the straight world might provide for dinner music. Those in the audience, unaccustomed to this kind of thing, were sure neither how to react to such classical sounds nor when to applaud. But putting on their best manners, showing how cool they could be, the audience caught the trio under the rubric of the word *groovy*. It was there so it had to be groovy, but still they were not sure. Finally, ignoring the obvious lack of improvisation, the use of written music, and the high seriousness and diligence of the performers, the audience refrained from committing the trio to the limbo of bummerland, relying on the cues of the flutist, his long hair and easy smile, to determine that this was or could be their kind of show.

Everyone there expected a good time, they might even have said later that it was a good time, but it was not. By no stretch of the imagination. Though the bands played long and loud, nothing was built. The audience and performers never came together to create a force larger than their individualities and their separatedness. Except for the drum solos of one group, which, like most drum solos, sounded good to most people and warranted a response simply for happening, the performances were listless. The crowd stood like unfeeling mutes, still, passive, dead. Nothing happened. Bludgeoned by the sound, stoned, the crowd had no vision of an ecstasy in which they might have to participate to create. All the energy in the hall was from Pacific Gas and Electric.

The success party was not without some feeling, as friends met and exchanged greetings, but few got more than high and tired. If joy was hard to find, it was perhaps that the ballroom harbored images of those who did not attend, all those who did not make it through the scene to become successful musicians, disc jockeys, film-makers, or promoters, those who did not have a chance to reconcile the new way of life with the great god Success.

Despite the presence of those who had prospered, those who had arrived, the ballroom had witnessed the lives of those with blown minds, hepatitis, syphilis, those who went home, cut their hair, went back to school or into the service, those who were busted, and those who died. And perhaps the hall itself, its soul enveloped in the mushroom curtains hanging from the ceiling, had a memory of the Hell's Angels' Birthday Party of months before, and levied a curse over all success achieved in the shadow of such death.

That night, despite the power and beauty of Janis Joplin, the event was marked by the pointless violence of those who were also in the fold. That night Angels, hundreds of them, choppers gleaming defiant to the gaze of the night employees across the street, entered the hall to assert failure and terrorism as a way of life. They had, in the piss on the floor and the stompings in the dining area, made their credo, their apologia, and their mea culpa.

The Angels eventually parted, roaring away into the night. The sound of the engines finally died, but the ballroom must have retained the evening in its floors and walls. For the Angels spoke not simply for themselves but for all the fragmentation and death of a movement that had borne at least its share of darkness. If success was the theme of this later gathering, if those who had made it came together for a good time, they could not wall out what was true, try as they might.

All this, needless to say, was the fault of no one in particular. But it was in the air, on the streets, and in the music. Even the bands sounded dated, like the old Jefferson Airplane. They had the San Francisco sound. But that style spoke for other days, days when everyone was younger, fresher, a little more original. It had been three years.

· 16 ·
Wasn't
That
a Mighty
Storm,
Lord?

Seeing life pass so quickly, watching the essence of our hopes threatened as we tried to render them real, witnessing the rate at which we learned the way of the world, I began to tell these stories. It was a sign of the good times that I saw myself as a singer of songs, a sign of the bad that I did not want to stop lest I, like Scheherazade, live only as long as I had one more tale.

The process of having shared such dreams, of having asked for so much, and having lived with these dreams as they were tested, yielded what we did not know would be such painful dissonances. Yet by the time I had found a written form for my stories I had gone past both exhilaration and despair. I had come out the other side of where I had once been, and felt that our lives were now a melody. The melody was in turn both joyous and sad, but what emerged without failure was the song. All was not lost.

We were always blessed with song, from the very start, when we felt that we had been deceived, when we were full of indignation and pointed the finger at a corrupt society. Songs recorded our progress from that point and led us on, songs by Dylan, the Beatles, the Stones, until we had a liturgy that was truly ours, resonating tones to celebrate our freedom and record our losses. And then, in time, these songs were no longer external. Rather, the very fabric of our lives, for better and for worse, contained the melodies we lived. We had come a long way.

To make affirmation a way of life, to get away from those who forever said no, and that part of ourselves, often proved impossible. Yet the endeavor was at times beyond saying, enormous, colossal. Denying dead forms, we had time and again the moment of first understanding, first freedom. There were so many flashes, surprises, realizations, epiphanies. For a time we were only ever more liberated, until, catching up to ourselves, we learned freedom from ignorance, and only then began to warrant all we had sought. We paid.

As a friend observed late in 1968, recording the latest turn of the screw, "not everybody who smokes dope gets high." Though it was an unkind reminder, we had in fact assumed, not so long before, not only that everyone could get high, but that their highs would be fundamentally similar (therefore shared) and essentially beneficent.

Our naïveté was, perhaps, beyond excuse. Our hurry to be free often made us greedy. Sure that we had been duped we rushed to make up for lost time, eager not only to be right but to have the satisfaction of flaunting our rightness. We were also unprepared for the implications of our discoveries—that the battles would be long and costly, that we too would carry our flaws, that we might not be able to straddle the growing distance between the life we were building and the life we wanted to reform or leave behind. We were slow to choose.

We wanted to play it both ways. We wanted the best of all possible worlds.

Those of us who remembered to look for more than an easy ride were searching for a home, working to locate or create an environment politically and interpersonally free from violence. Unable to relate to our homeland, we came to see ourselves as outlanders if not outlaws, and were considered both alien and criminal by those who felt more at home—those who owned homes—in this land. At our best we sought peace, not the *pax* of the Romans, the order and suppression of force, but *shalom*, the peace of full expression, the plenitude of the whole. At our worst we sought out the *Sturm und Drang*, unwilling to settle for quieter resolutions, eager for a historic capitulation, large screen and full color, ours if it could not be theirs.

Beyond the pale, planning now to rework the larger society, now to escape it, unsure of whether we were seditious, radically patriotic, or expatriate, we marched, picketed, demonstrated, gathered, organized, conspired, and fled. Ever more on our own, we struggled to find shelter.

There were, of course, varying degrees of homelessness, and some were either farther along the path or safe, for the moment, at some way station. Two men whom I came to know were so determined in their quest, were so cast adrift, that they lived for over a year sleeping in a different place each night, calling around to find a spare bed or sofa, walking, hitching, getting a lift on to the next stop, consuming ever more of their energies in simply finding protection from the damp cold of the night.

Had they wanted there is no question that they could have found some haven, a room in a house, a cheap apartment, something. Yet they were driven to keep moving, always around Berkeley, wanderers ever so close to home. It was as if some oracle had brought them just out of reach and then, perversely, left them perpetually on the verge of discovery. They knew, they were certain, that what they sought was bound to appear, any day, but moved in the fear that they already had missed it, or had somehow misread what the oracle said.

Though they never met, each logged nights in my apartment, circling the living room before bedding down, trying to mold some private space out of so public a room, trying to shape yet another nest from such inhospitable material. The morning after, observing the schedule of seasoned transients, they always left by noon, unable to give up their search, worn by the journey, looking carefully for some sign, fearful that they would misinterpret the omen when it appeared, if it appeared.

They speak for those times, for all of us, in both their effort to find a place to live, to be, to feel right, and in the self-imposed terms of their struggle. The endeavor itself and the absence of guides precluded any short cuts on the path that led us from what we chose to leave behind, the path we followed in the hope that it would lead us where we said we wished to go. Pilgrims all, our progress was slow, the maps obscure, the obstacles many, our temptations and weaknesses beyond number.

Many of us succumbed with terror to the realization that this was no side trip, no jaunt. Yet for those on their own, feeding too well on despair and confusion after the early exhilaration of cutting loose had waned, some succor could be taken from the knowledge itself. Still, only the very strong, the very sure and very trusting, persisted past fear and fatigue to leave behind pride, envy, sloth, anger, lust, avarice, and gluttony. Often forlorn, often totally at a loss to know the way, we laughed, sang, ran, crawled, stumbled, clawed, and dragged our way onward, more than a few lost at every turn.

Along the way I brought myself low, and had occasion to confront my own folly and pray for reprieve. I came also to the point where the tide swept me clean, where I was carried on its bosom, washed into the sea of lives like my own. Time became of no moment. I began to feel less special. I shrived and confessed myself; I made a private journey to the India of my being, washed in the Ganges, and passed my way through the millions as a brother in time.

If in singing my songs I had come to see myself as Orpheus, if I had had my moments of dance, of love, of victory, then I like him descended into hell, and like him entered into a dream, drawn into my memories by a song. Like Orpheus I had asked too much, lost, learned, and in the process found my true songs.

Now I, with those who spun on the circle of which I have spoken, are some of the people, a few of the two-thousand million. Some things we have lost, some prices we have paid, some things we have learned. In that dialectic of change which has been ours, we who flew into the sun so many times, those of us who live on, work now to build, to fashion new wings, to craft them with more skill. Better prepared, we will go farther, to better places.

Those years, those moments, slip away. Another generation, only several years later, inherits and transmutes the changes we went through. Perforce we move on. Who does know where the time goes?

Life, the circle game, of course moves on, round and round, simply demanding the inevitable prices. Even so, countless apocalypses have flashed and passed on, but we are still here. For those of you who have come this far, for those of you who survive to raise a glass to the good and the evil, for those of you who now look for some separate peace, I offer one more story, and a final enjoinder.

· 17 ·
John

Let me take you down, or, sixty years on.

Where have you spent most of your life?
In institutions.
Did you have a happy life as a child?
No.
How many years of school did you attend?
Eight grades.
Did you lose interest in school?
Yes.
Why?
_____

At what age did you leave home?
_____

Why?

Are you married?
No.
Do you have a common-law wife?
No.
Do you have children?
No.
Were you ever in the military forces?
No.
Do you like to travel?
Yes.
Why?
To see historical places.
Do you have convulsions?
No.
Do you have dizzy spells?
No.
Do you have fainting spells?
No.
Do you have severe mental shock?
No.
Are you nervous?
No.
Are you excitable?
No.
Do you think you have a bad temper?
No.
How many times have you been arrested?
Quite a few.
Are you guilty this time?
Yes.
What did you do on the "outside"?
Hospital orderly.
Were you incarcerated before?
Yes.

When?
1940–50, 1950–52, 1953–56, 1957–64, 1965–69.
Do you have any sexual problems?
No.
How do you feel in the morning?
Fresh.
Do you have dreams?
No.
Do you have nightmares?
No.
Do you have any bitter or painful memories?
Yes. Too much time.
Do you bite your nails?
No.
Are you moody?
No.
Are you happy now?
No.
Are you unhappy now?
Yes.
What is your main worry?
Old age.
Are you too ambitious?
No.
Are you suicidal?
No.
Are you desirous of success?
No.
Do you drink?
Seldom.
Do you play poker?
No.
Do you roll dice?
No.
Do you bet on the races?

No.
Do you use drugs?
No.
Were you ever in the Boy Scouts?
No.
Were you ever in the YMCA?
Yes.
Do you have a religion here?
No.
With whom do you plan to live when you get out?
Myself.

Consider now this old man, imagine the waiting he had done in his life, the waiting in county jails, the waiting in bird cages behind courtroom doors, the waiting for meals, for directions, for the day of release. Consider too that he had lost the ability or the will to stay away from prison. A threshold had been crossed; a final vital iota of resilience had been eroded or bludgeoned away. Catechisms which inveighed against the heresy of manhood had been whispered too many times.

John had spent perhaps thirty years of his life inside the walls on various sentences ("bits," they were called, pieces of a whole), and waited once again for the end of his present term, watching each unit of time pass by, waiting until one bearing his name presented itself, all in good time, of course. In observing the flow he had become deft at gauging the rate—a timekeeper. Someone ventured that it had to be at least three-thirty, time for chow. "No," John said, "only three-fifteen." The man did not argue the point, though the discussion itself might have carried them through several minutes. No, his opinion of the time was an ingénue's query posed to an expert. John had survived a long time, had done a lot of time, and was generally credited with being an expert on time, time-honored, as it were.

In the process of walking off each segment of his life span

he had reduced his life to order and control, to anticipating and rolling with the routine, to riding the breakers of each wave of time, and had learned never to offend anyone, hack or con. Since neither silence nor neutrality could guarantee safety he appeased everyone, every last man. He had learned to place himself at the very bottom of the peck order, a threat to absolutely no one. So harmless had he become that he could occasionally expect to receive the largesse of those who competed for so much more from life. A soft job from the lieutenant, a good seat in the movie hall, these were the perquisites of total abnegation.

In learning to wait, in learning to wait without ever giving offense, his life in words had been reduced to one form or another of genuflection. "How are ya?" or "How ya doing?" always sure to be offered with a blank smile. In addition to the salutations he communicated to all possible enemies (that is, to everyone), he had several other catch phrases the essence of which had long since escaped him, rhetorical questions, imprecations, and requests which had in time long past ceased to convey any expectation of response.

"Figure that one out." He said the phrase randomly. It popped up at any time, after any event, with any idea. Once the phrase had articulated surprise, was at least a statement of the impossibility of expecting anything reasonable to occur. But over time it had become no more than a rote phrase. He had reduced it all to that. Any why not? It had worked. He lived to say the words long after Al Capone, Shorty McGee, Red Wilson, Clyde Barrow, long after men bigger, tougher, and smarter than he had been laid to rest. "Figure that one out."

Well, he had stopped trying to figure anything out. It was all pretty obvious, obviously insane. The phrase, therefore, was not only not an imperative, but was uttered with each new shock or for just any occurence, without hope for any form of instrumental understanding. Now formula, the message of the phrase was nonetheless clear: it isn't really very hard to figure anything out, and when you do, it would have been better if you hadn't, and you can't do anything about it anyway.

In the same way, like a human toaster, he continually popped up with "Oh my God" or "God bless us and save us." These words (his finger outlining the cross) must once have functioned as a reaction to some moment of terror, some blow that his system could not and would not absorb. There had been, however, so many blows that the words had become declensions of verbs the meaning of which he had long since forgotten. That horror had elicited the same response from him so many times that the phrases had been reduced to babble. They came to take a place as choral elements in his ceaseless litany of horror stories, tales which in the telling became tokens of his capacity for survival, tales which warded off the silence he had not tasted for so many years, of which he had become so afraid.

The silence, such as it may have been, vanished at the age of seventeen when he began his institutional life, when he entered a universe in which there was not one corner in which a man could be alone, in which he could for one moment be free from the breathing, thinking, and yearning of hundreds of other men. Nor could there be isolation from the ordered discipline. Even thought crimes were punished, if only by oneself. Not even psychological privacy was to be asked for. It required a battle to set up a wall within those outside walls, to maintain anything that was even potentially contraband, not to accept the institution's definition of its best interests. It was a battle one only foolishly engaged in, and always lost. Nothing, not even memories of another time, were to be smuggled inside. Those dreams of a past which did manage to scale the walls faded almost without notice.

It was early, then, that John gave up his privacy. Understanding that it would be easier to live if he had no thoughts of his own, he abandoned them too. Oh, to be sure, he had his

205

desires, but he lost the capacity to dream for more than a better or worse dinner, to hunger for more than two packs of cigarettes instead of one. Deprivation became a way of life, he yielded almost everything except life itself to be spared further pain, and talked incessantly to fill the vacuum. Rather than face the void, or perhaps just to make sure that no one could take offense from his silence, he talked without pause, his stories culled from years inside and from brief vacations as a free man, all augmented by stories from the street that reached him through the walls.

Thus, in just this way, he could describe the shanking (the knifing) of a man in prison, how the murderers waited until the guard had passed before they threw the body from the fifth tier, and he could then pass directly from this, save for "Figure that one out" or "Oh, my God," to a story about the man who killed his neighbors and was charged with intent to commit necrophilic acts. Over time, through time, doing time, marking time, wasting time, killing time, in no time, time after time, serving time, out of time, for the time of his life, John became a walking encyclopedia of the macabre. The stories offered as anecdote and entertainment, these timeworn stories were the only ones he knew.

Having seen so many forms of mayhem and murder, having lived for so long with the fear of offending someone despite his own best efforts, having reduced himself to being a creature who claimed almost nothing except the right to request to go on living—having done this and still having to live with the fear that he might be sleeping one night when some lunatic came creeping up on him in the dark to hold court on him with an iron bar, living with this fear—he had come to see the outside, ever only a mirage, as simply more of the same.

There were brothers who did not write and a mother who did not visit, whores in Steubenville, Ohio, and the daily paper. He read to keep up with the deaths, murders, rapes, and scandals that comprised the news. So familiar was he with all this, so unable was he to discern any fundamental difference between the quality of life inside and outside, that he spoke of people from both worlds with equal familiarity, mingling the stories of each without notice, blending both so completely that in any real sense he had lived them all. Given his presentation, it was hard to argue that the worlds were different.

The flow of stories was endless, from the man who was a hero at sea, and then murdered someone, and turned out to have sunk the boat on purpose, from him directly to the guy who set his mattress on fire in the cell and they left him there and he died like a rat, which led to the dead racoon on the highway, which brought him to "Heaven forbid it should be one of us," and the fingers outlined the cross.

He could perform, and would take you through memory lane before you could ask him (or rather command him—no one asked John for anything except the time of day): "For there on the floor, on top of the whore, lay Dangerous Dan McGrew." "Dancing with my shadow, making believe it's you." "I walk along this street of sorrow, this boulevard of broken dreams." "You call everybody darling, everybody calls you darling too." "There is a gold mine in the sky." "It's just a shanty in old shanty town."

When the songs ran out he'd tell you about Two-Ton Gilento out of Paterson (John never forgot a pedigree), or about the Titanic, or about George Rogers, who said that he'd eat so much that they wouldn't be able to get him into the electric chair, but they did. Or he could offer a little quick patriotism, stories about how he made uniforms inside the walls during the war, sagas about how we licked the Japs.

Over time he had become a pet, a housebroken animal, no danger to anyone, just aware enough of the fragility of his environment to remember to be ingratiating. All he asked was five dollars a month and he would do that labor, and never never forget to tip his hat and give you top of the morning. Or you could take away that five dollars, you could do anything short of killing him, since nothing could induce John to risk any change for the worse.

Someone once decided to tease John, or just to tell him the kind of truth that has no right to be uttered. "John," the man said, "you'll get out but you'll just come back again." For a moment, just a moment, John faced the void once more, tasted the silence, and was silent. To come back would be to die inside the walls. He started to say no, a word he had long since learned not to use. Forced to see the horror again, however, he began to form the word on his lips. And then, recovering, he grimaced, smiled, and said, "Yeah, figure that one out." Yeah, figure that one out. Oh my God. God help us and save us. God forbid it should be one of us.

· 18 ·
Afterword

"I'm alive, ain't that news? I've been livin' with the blues."

I have told you something of pioneer days, the way it was, where we were. Enough of the past tense. Let us proceed. There is a calm after every storm. On our circle we pause now to take a sad song and make it better. Our friends, we find, are all aboard. We sit down to eat. A cup full of happiness, a great big slice of life, one peace of mind. We breathe deep, and let it out to let it in. The lost are, for the moment, found. To be sure, we compromise, but there must be time for some quiet living.

We are experienced now, and we know it. Only a few years ago our effort was to point the finger, to break from the past, to widen the circle of possibilities. This we have done. What confronts us still is the implementation of our tempered hopes and costly understanding. Positions defined, the task is to develop vehicles for life, without which we have only self-righteousness and truths which, repeated too many times, become something less than true.

Perhaps some day there will be a final telling of these stories, and, if so, the book will have to open like a music box, silver lid pulling back, two silver butlers holding a curtain between them flipping up as the saraband begins. As the dance continues the two butlers, moving stiffly, will pull the curtain back, step by halting step, and, as the open space widens, we will see unfolding a panorama, blue skies and white clouds. We will glide through this space, and, looking down, we will see the peaks of great mountains. We will descend. Far below, in the valleys, no more than specks of color, we will see our people. "There they are," we'll say.

It will be a fairy tale, the narrative voice quite avuncular, the tone of the whole a magic show. The words will no longer have symbolic meaning, but will be simply sounds, feelings. Then there will be only silence, and the lives themselves.

Until that time, in the interval between those lives and these stories, we must move on. It does not take long to rekindle the fire. For those of you who do not see the way, for those of you who like us all must now and again pay the piper, I send you this troubador's song. Here are the words. I know you'll find the melody.

Speed, bonny boat, like a bird on the wing,
Onward, the sailors cry,
Carry the lad who's born to be king,
Over the sea to Skye.
Loud the winds howl, loud the waves roar,
Thunderclouds rend the air.
Baffled our foe, stand on the shore,
Follow they will not dare, oh

Speed, bonny boat, like a bird on the wing,
Onward the sailors cry.
Carry the lad who's born to be king,
Over the sea to Skye.